Dispelling
THE CLOUDS
...A DESPERATE SOCIAL EXPERIMENT

WILMA DERKSEN

Library and Archives Canada Cataloguing in Publication
Derksen, Wilma
Dispelling the Clouds: Desperate Social Experiment / Wilma Derksen
BIO026000 Biography & Autobiography / Personal Memoirs
BIO032000 Biography & Autobiography / Social Activists
SOC016000 Social Science / Human Services
ISBN: 978-1-7770080-1-7
Dispelling the Clouds: A Desperate Social Experiment
Copyright © 2020 by Wilma Derksen
Second Edition November 2020

Books available through:
Amity Publishers
www.amitypublishers
email: amitypublishers@gmail.com
For more information:
Telephone/cell - 204 770 9272

Dedicated to my husband, my children,
their spouses and our grandchildren
Love you all

CONTENTS

Preface

Experimentation means trying something new. I find it amazing how many well-known people have believed that life is an experiment.

Marcus Aurelius – "Nothing has such power to broaden the mind as the ability to investigate systematically and truly all that comes under thy observation in life."

William Blake – "The true method of knowledge is experiment."

Thomas Alva Edison – "The real measure of success is the number of experiments that can be crowded into twenty-four hours."

Albert Einstein – "No amount of experimentation can ever prove me right; a single experiment can prove me wrong."

Ralph Waldo Emerson – "All life is an experiment."

H. G. Wells – "Heresies are experiments in man's unsatisfied search for truth."

An experiment in science is a complex procedure carried out to support, or refute a hypothesis. If the experiment does not work, then one needs to come up with another hypothesis.

A life experiment is similar. We want to see if something works as planned and desired. We want to get one step closer to the objective truth.

Yet life is uncertain. Very few people have lives that are exactly as they planned or predicted. There are twists and turns in the journey that not even the most forward thinking can predict. We can only plan and then take action. We cannot really know. In this sense, all of life is an experiment. Not taking action is an experiment too.

What if we live life as an experiment? What will we do differently?

I think we take more risks. If experiments are all about discovery and growth, we're willing to do all sorts of things we might be embarrassed to do otherwise.

And that's exactly what I found myself doing. I didn't know it – but for most of my life, I was living an experiment.

Consciously or unconsciously it was just an experiment... motivated by desperation.

INTRODUCTION

Something was on our bed….

We didn't have words for it.

It was moving, writhing – defying us.

Cliff saw a reptilian image with a circling tail. The eyes were hooded – a lazy serpent stare…lifeless.

I saw it more as a voracious, wolf-like dog – snarling, fierce and otherworldly. I have a latent fear of dogs and this resembled my worst nightmare.

The presence was shapeshifting before our very eyes….

We both knew it was a figment of our imaginations. It was as if our fears were appearing before our very eyes in this mysterious form, glaring at us from our own bed – a ghostly omen from the dark side.

It wasn't real.

Yet, it was real. We both saw something on our bed – a black mirage, a cloud of something that hovered like a dark presence, with magical abilities to change into the shape of whatever we feared the most.

PART I

Chapter 1
GYMNASIUM

The school gymnasium was filled with squirming high school adolescents – a collective audience of hormones – a challenge for any speaker even at the best of times. And this was the most challenging time of all – right after lunch.

They wiggled, they talked, and they threw things at each other – until he walked on to the stage.

He placed his hands on the podium, and immediately a hush fell over the gym. There was something about him.

He embodied the indescribable power of someone who is exceptionally confident, composed, and ready to take on anything the world wants to throw at him. We all felt it – we all knew it.

"I am René Durocher," he said in a thick French-Canadian accent.

He scanned the audience.

"When I was a young boy, a priest came to our house. He told my mother that I had great potential. He said that I would become a great person someday. He just wasn't sure whether it would be a great prime minister – or a great criminal."

He paused. No one was talking, throwing things, or punching anyone anymore. You could have heard a pin drop in that full gymnasium.

"I chose to become a great criminal."

He paused to let his words sink in. Then he added quietly, "And I became one of the best."

No one moved after that – he had the students in the palm of his hand as he began to tell his story.

"I had been released from prison only three months prior, and I was already planning my next bank robbery. This time it was a bank in Rosemont – the biggest. There were four of us involved – three of us to rob the bank and one to drive the getaway car.

"We parked on the street in front of the bank. We pulled nylon stockings over our faces as masks and ran in.

"I was the last one to leave the car, following my partners with the machine gun in my hands, covering them so that they would be safe.

"Once inside the bank, I started barking orders, 'Everybody on the ground. Don't move, or I will kill you.'

"I fired a round of bullets into the ceiling with my M1 rifle they used in Vietnam. I also had a spare gun, a Mark III Commando with a double clip strapped to my waist. I walked the floor yelling and swearing at the people to lie down and not move, threatening that if they didn't, they were all going to die. And I meant it – and they knew it."

He paused. He was pacing the stage – we felt it. He didn't have a gun – but the way he walked....

His voice was low. "We had to control the scene. It was the only way we could get the money. We treated it like a job."

He stood very still. "Because I was the one with the machine gun, I was the boss."

None of us doubted it.

Then his voice changed, dropping low, speaking to us as confidantes – almost whispering. "As the boss, I am the one who is looking around – covering the other two as they went about their business. We have only seconds to do our work. I'm the one who keeps my eye on the time. When I say it's time, they have to stop, so I'm the one who is tasked with keeping my eye on the time. When I say go, we go.

"My two partners were jumping over the counters and scooping up the money from the tills. In no time, their bags were full. Money was spilling....

"They were fast.

"When they had emptied as many tills as I thought reasonable, I called to them that their time was up! They stopped everything, and we raced out of the building, leaving the people still screaming and lying on the floor.

"Our driver was ready for us. The doors were already open, and all the windows were open."

He paused.

"Because I was covering my partners with the gun, I was the last one to reach the car.

"Even though the back door was ajar, it was not open enough for me to get in, so I fumbled with it. Our driver was anxious and was already gunning the motor. I had to do a running jump into that moving car – just barely making it."

It felt as if we were with him – in an action movie. Our hearts were racing.

"There hadn't been a moment to spare. We had done it in the allotted time – two minutes – and we had to get out of there – fast.

"Already we felt that relief of a job well done. We were already millionaires. We were about to celebrate when a huge, bulletproof City of Montreal truck pulled up in front of us – blocking us.

"Police!

"Using a bullhorn, the cops were ordering us, 'Surrender! We have you surrounded!'

"I yelled at our driver, 'Fuck them. We are not surrendering.'

"I pulled out my pistol and put it to his head, 'If you don't go, I am going to kill you.'

"He drove like a maniac and managed to get around the truck.

"The bullets were beginning to fly, so I started shooting back. I started acting like a wild man. I still don't know what came over me. I was shooting at anything and everything.

"My partner, who was sitting right in front of me, got hit – a bullet right in his head. In slow motion, I saw him just slump down in his seat.

"My other partner, who was sitting with me in the back of the car, was also shooting from his side of the car and got hit by two bullets that came from the trunk and hit him in the back.

"But nothing was going to stop me. I kept yelling at the driver, 'You have to keep going, or I'll kill you.' But eventually, the car came to a stop. The cops had used a shotgun – and he had been shot through the windshield into his face. He was slumped over the wheel.

"I picked up my automatic M1 because my Mark III was empty, jumped out of the car and started to run, and run, and shoot. I didn't care that there were people on the street – screaming. I would have killed anyone in my way. I didn't care. I was a maniac. I just wanted to get away. They were right after me.

"Those cops were motivated. We had robbed a few banks before, and they knew by our style that this was a repeat job. They were frustrated that they hadn't been able to capture us, so they wanted us stopped even if it meant killing us on the job.

"Because I knew the cops wanted to kill us, I thought, 'If I'm going to die, they are going to die before I do.' I hated anyone in authority.

"The cops surrounded me by a school wall. I turned my machine gun on myself, and I tried to kill myself, right there on the spot. But the gun jammed.

"They jumped on me and took me down.

"They put the handcuffs on me and took me to the Parthenais Jail. It was a brand-new jail at the time. All I could think of was my partners.

"As it turned out, the driver, who got the shotgun pellets in his face, was OK. My other partner was killed.

"I didn't understand it. 'How the hell was it not me? How the hell was I not hit?' All the bullets came right through the vehicle. 'Why?'

"I blamed the cops. You always blame the shooter. Later, when they counted the holes in the car, there were seventy-two. I don't know how many bullets passed straight through – we'll never know – but they counted seventy-two bullet holes in the car."

He then described his time in prison, and then at the very end, he said that he had changed.

"My wife, the mother of my two children, told me that if I didn't change my ways, I would never see my children again. I was serving time in Prince Albert, and I knew that she would do as she said. And that's when I woke up. I loved my children…."

Then, just as he had convinced us that he was the worst criminal in his time, he did a complete turnaround and proceeded to convince us – just as persuasively – that the choice to be a criminal was the worst choice he had made. He had wasted his life.

He talked about the cost, the regrets, and his remorse.

By the time he walked off the stage, the students looked stunned and dazed. They had slid down in their chairs, limp as dish rags.

Everyone saw a man. I saw a warrior cloud thundering….

Avoiding everyone, I slipped out of the building, found my car, and drove slowly back to my office.

No sooner had I settled behind my desk when a colleague from down the hall stuck her head into my office. "I heard that you were at a restorative justice conference with Durocher – that is so amazing. The organizers told me that both of you were riveting. They were so thrilled to have you both at their restorative justice school conference. Imagine having the most well-known victim in the city – together with a notorious criminal – telling their story on the same day. Amazing."

Then before I could answer – she was gone.

Her words rang in my ears.... "Most well-known victim in the city – together with a notorious criminal?"

"Notorious."

I kept hearing the word "notorious" over and over again.

Was I being billed in the same sentence together with a notorious criminal – who had once been the most wanted man in Canada?

I couldn't get her words out of my mind.

How had I gotten here?

Chapter 2
STRANGER

I just sat there at my desk, immobilized for a long time, staring out my office window, watching the restless clouds pile up on each other. The dark clouds were being pushed to the bottom as they rumbled by with the wind hurrying them along. But they were beginning to drag with the weight of their precipitation.

Would it be rain or snow? Perhaps snow mixed with rain. Deadly on the road.

It had dipped below -20C earlier in the week, and there was a good layer of snow on the ground already, but it was milder today – fluctuations typical of November in Winnipeg.

I couldn't help but remember another November, similar in weather – eight years ago.

It was as if I was there again – down in the basement of our house. The telephone rang. It was Candace, our thirteen-year-old daughter, who was attending a private school down the street, asking for a ride. I was up against a writing deadline. I promised her that if she walked home we would pick up all the junk food she needed to make it a party weekend.

"No problem," she giggled as she hung up. I turned back to my work – losing track of time.

When I had eventually emerged from the downstairs, project completed, Candace had not come home.

Frantically, I had packed our other children, Odia, nine, and Syras, two, into the car, and headed down Talbot Avenue to retrace her steps. There was no sign of her on the street – or of anyone. Students were all safe at home by now.

I then drove further down Henderson Highway to pick my husband up from his Camp Arnes office, and then we drove home in desperate silence, praying all the way, hoping Candace would be home when we got back.

But the house was empty.

We called everyone we knew. No one knew anything.

We alerted the police and expected them to put out an immediate missing person alert, but they weren't at all worried. They said she was probably just another weekend runaway.

We knew she wasn't. She was expecting her best friend to come in from Gimli – and Candace was all about her friends. She would never let Heidi down.

Candace's body was found seven weeks later, and we were asked to drive to Seven Oaks Hospital, northwest of where we lived, to identify her body.

It was the longest, hardest drive of our lives.

Once there, they briefed us on the details. They told us her body would be allowed to thaw and that, even though she might have died on the evening she disappeared, her death certificate would record January 17, 1985, as the date of her death.

We nodded mechanically.

"How did she die?" I asked.

"We can't be sure until after the autopsy, but her hands and feet were tied. Right now, it looks as if she might have frozen to death."

"Who would take her and just tie her up and leave her to die? She didn't have any real enemies."

"It could have been sex. Tying. Bonding is often sexual," she said slowly.

I nodded.

9

By the time we reached our home, friends were already waiting for us. They had heard it over the news and were there with food in hand.

We invited them in – we needed them.

Together with them, we swung dizzily between relief that we had found her, relief that the frantic search was over, to the pain of the realization that she would never come home again.

And then….

Murder is life changing. This was when I had acquired the label "victim," but then something equally life changing happened.

Someone came to visit us.

It was around ten o'clock the same night that Candace's body was found when the doorbell rang.

I opened the front door cautiously, only to find a stranger dressed in black – blending in with the darkness of the night.

"I've come to tell you what to expect," he said. "I, too, am a parent of a murdered child."

By this time, my husband had joined me, and we invited the man to sit at the kitchen table with us and a couple of friends who had offered to stay the night. We were debriefing the day over a piece of warm cherry pie.

I cut him a piece of the pie – comfort food.

He sat down and began to tell the story of his daughter's murder, beginning from the moment he had learned of the murder, followed by the intensity of the investigation, which included an arrest and ended with a detailed account of the two trials. He had an amazing memory for every graphic detail.

We had followed his story in the news. His daughter had been killed in a donut shop three years previously. The police had charged a suspect, and the trial had been in the news for the past two years. I hadn't followed it closely, but even from the headlines, I had sensed that the victim's family was bitterly angry and traumatized by the whole process.

The murder had a consequence, he said.

He told us how the murder had destroyed his life, his health, his ability to work and concentrate. He listed the medications he was taking. It was a show and tell. He even pulled out the bottles to show us and lined them up on the table – a string of evidence. Then he told us about the incessant media coverage, as he piled his own little black books on the table. The same little black books the reporters used. He had recorded everything, probably in more detail than they had. And then he paused. "I've even lost the memory of my daughter."

I could tell. He hadn't said one word about his daughter. He had spent the entire time talking about the accused, the justice system, and his overwhelming trauma – nothing about his daughter.

"This is a warning. I'm telling you this to let you know what lies ahead," he said over and over again like a prophet of doom.

And we just sat there – all of us – numb.

It was two hours later – well after midnight – when he had finally finished his cherry pie, picked up his pile of notebooks, and took his leave.

With a collective sigh of relief, we closed the door behind him – expecting that the dark presence that had come in with him would leave with him, but it didn't.

Our friends retired to their bedroom downstairs, and Cliff and I went upstairs to our bedroom.

Quiet – so very quiet. The children were sleeping.

We opened the door – and stopped.

I remember standing immobilized at the door of our bedroom with my husband for some time – looking at this thing.

Something was on our bed….

We didn't have words for it.

It was moving, writhing – defying us.

Cliff saw a reptilian image with a circling tail. The eyes were hooded – a lazy serpent stare…lifeless.

I saw it more as a voracious, wolf-like dog – snarling, fierce and otherworldly. I have a latent fear of dogs and this resembled my worst nightmare.

The presence was shapeshifting before our very eyes….

We both knew it was a figment of our imaginations. It was as if our fears were appearing before our very eyes in this mysterious form, glaring at us from our own bed – a ghostly omen from the dark side.

It wasn't real.

Yet, it was real. We both saw something on our bed – a black mirage, a cloud of something that hovered like a dark presence, with magical abilities to change into the shape of whatever we feared the most.

We looked with horror at each other. If the man is right…our lives are over. He had said, "The impact of murder is more deadly than the murder itself."

And this was the evidence – this thing.

What to do?

Desperation! We felt a huge desperation. We were too exhausted for this thing.

We looked at the creature again – growing – slithering back and forth – defying us, daring us to come closer, daring us to go to bed with him.

Yet we were not without resources….

We had been taught how to deal with trauma…. We had been taught there was a way to move through horror – even the horror of murder.

We would not engage with this thing.

"We will forgive…," we said to each other. We agreed.

We turned to challenge the thing on our bed.

"We will forgive…," we said again, defying it.

It was stunned. It slowly started to shrink – shrivel – and then it simply evaporated.

We waited for a bit – barely able to believe our words had that much power.

As we prepared for bed – it did not return. We noticed a tiny, dark cloud in the corner – a kind of reminder of the trauma and grief. But we expected that. We could live with that – as long as it wasn't on the bed.

And then we fell asleep – a minor miracle, after all we had been through.

But it didn't end there.

A few days after Candace's body was found, we organized a press conference to show our appreciation to the city of Winnipeg and thank them for being there for us. We held it at the school Candace had attended.

The press showed up in full Winnipeg force.

It was in the cafeteria – we sat behind a desk.

Cliff began by reading a formal letter of appreciation.

They had not only helped us look for our daughter, but they had also responded to our new passion which was to support other families looking for their children. With their generosity, we were able to initiate a Child Find in Manitoba.

Since Candace was all about friends, and since Winnipeg had become one massive friend, in keeping with her memory we simply invited everyone to Candace's memorial service. It was a gesture of appreciation – I didn't think anyone would want to attend a memorial service. But after the announcement, our friends who were helping us organize things, and who knew better, immediately booked the largest church in town.

After the lights went down and the reporters were closing their little black notebooks, one of the reporters sitting closer to the back asked us how we felt about the perpetrator – the person who had murdered our daughter.

Cliff and I paused.

We didn't know how to answer that question. Frankly, we hadn't given much thought to the murderer. From what the police officers had told us, we assumed it was a "street person" – and a stranger to us.

We were much more preoccupied with the shadow of that dark, reptilian presence, but how do you explain that to a reporter? How do you describe the power to disengage? How do you explain how we were choosing an alternative route – the radical path of forgiveness?

We didn't even know how to explain it to ourselves, much less do it.

Without thinking, I said, "I am going to forgive."

Cliff, always sure of himself, was able to say, "I have forgiven."

There were no more questions.

The next day the headlines in the newspaper were all about our choice to forgive.

And it was that word that sent me careening down an entirely different path than most parents of murdered children.

It was that word….

Chapter 3
BRANDED

The bank of clouds laboriously dragged by outside my window – seething and writhing with inner weight.

I stared at it, and then it stared back with that shapeshifting face of a serpent, a haunting apparition, its eyes – lifeless, brooding.

The eyes were seeing something...and I knew what it was.

It was attracted to the storm within me. It was attracted to all of the storms around me – and there had been so many.

But it wasn't only my personal struggles. There was a whole justice system out there.

It really was the perfect storm weather-wise – inside and outside.

Shortly after the press conference for our daughter's murder, an article was published in the *Windsor Star*. The title was: *No revenge sought in murder*, Winnipeg CP - Canadian Press.

The journalist had begun the article by quoting Cliff.

"'We would like to know who the person or persons are so we could share hopefully a love that seems to be missing in that person's life,' said Cliff Derksen embracing the Mennonite beliefs that dictate the way from revenge."

Then the journalist had interviewed a University of Manitoba sociologist who said that the beliefs expressed by Cliff were exceptional but not surprising given that, in this case, they came from a religious place – Mennonite, to be exact.

"I understand the Mennonite religion quite well, and I expect that this would be their reaction," he wrote. "But I sure wouldn't expect it from anyone else who didn't have these religious beliefs.... Something like 70 to 80 percent of Canadians want capital punishment – and the vast majority of them have never been touched by a murderer – even remotely."

The writer then said that he had spoken to non-Mennonites who were afraid of our response. They believed that if the pursuit of Candace's assailant was not carried through to its end, it would only prompt others to kill.

The article ended with this quote. "The Derksens are saying 'forgive him,' and they're saying 'what you're doing is encouraging other people to do that again in the future.'"

First of all, I was surprised that there were up to eighty percent of Canadians who didn't agree with us – that was disconcerting. We were unpopular.

I felt it too. So I wanted to explain – defend myself. I started to put my story onto paper at the same time as I was being asked to tell my story. I accepted all speaking engagements. People wanted to know about forgiveness – so I told them about the stranger at the door.

But this had only helped to polarize public opinion.

I remember feeling so isolated. I didn't belong anywhere. I started to look for a place to be accepted. That's when I received a call from someone who introduced himself as president of a newly established survivors support group, called Family Survivors of Homicide, comprised mainly of parents of murdered children. I was immediately interested.

Even over the telephone, he was warm, inviting and seemed to understand the issues of murder that no one else seemed to understand, so I debriefed with him – I think almost monthly at first.

As president, he invited me to attend the meetings, but I declined. I was too busy to fit one more thing into my schedule. I had landed full-time work as a journalist for a denominational paper. I was supporting my husband in his demanding career as a camp director while mothering our two remaining children who were now ages eleven and six. In addition to that, we had been involved with the establishment of a swimming pool at Camp Arnes in Candace's name, and helped found Child Find Manitoba. I was intent on doing good.

Then when I resigned from Child Find, the next time the president called, I found myself listening with new interest. Was this it? Was this my next step? Was this survivors support group a way of learning about the shadow side of murder? Did everyone have a trauma beast in their lives, or was it just us? At the end of the telephone conversation, I asked if I could join the group – and meet everyone face to face.

"Sure…." There was a long pause at the other end of the telephone line. "We've wanted you to join our group."

There was another long, awkward pause. "But we have talked about you recently and decided that we needed to reconsider our invitation, so I need to check with the group first to see if it is okay with them…. I'll get back to you."

I was stunned.

I had thought he'd be excited – he had been so warm and welcoming over the telephone – but now to hear his hesitancy was devastating.

Why did he have to ask his group if I could join? What was it about me that was unacceptable? If I didn't belong to this exclusive group – where did I belong? I was running out of options….

I hung up, feeling very rejected and hurt. I really didn't think I would hear from him again – and I wasn't sure what I wanted anymore. I would find another way.

But he called a few days later.

"I talked to the group," he began casually. "And they said that they would let you join our group on one condition…." He paused again…. "That you lose the word forgiveness."

Lose the word forgiveness?

I was shocked.

17

Yes, of course, I would lose the word forgiveness…for them I would.

Yet I couldn't.

Even though I kept the agreement, and I never talked about it in the group – the word itself would not go away. I needed it constantly as a way to fend off the clouds that stalked the group.

We were all caught in a nation-wide perfect storm – and we didn't realize it. This was when the entire justice system was being challenged in a new way.

Let me give you the background….

In the seventies, Canada had been involved in a heavy debate on the pros and cons of capital punishment. In 1976, the House of Commons abolished hanging by a majority of six votes. It was only in 1998 that Canada finally eliminated the death penalty for military members, becoming a fully abolitionist country when it came to executions.

So, we were right in the middle of the discussion – a discussion that had huge implications! It played havoc with our natural justice instinct of "a life for a life." Without a death penalty, there was no hope of resolution for us as parents of murdered children. Murder was the ultimate crime. We tend to want to eradicate our worst fears – and anyone that harms our children needs to be removed – permanently – from this world. Now without the hope of capital punishment, this safety net was gone. How can you come to a place of justice satisfaction when someone so dear to you – irreplaceable – has been taken violently from you, and there is no justice? If the killer continues to live – every breath they take becomes an insult to the life they've taken.

This was the reaction of those who had experienced murder so it shouldn't come as a surprise that, in 1980, the Criminal Justice System began to see they needed to address this need, and established a Federal/Provincial Task Force on Justice for Victims of Crime.

Three years after being established, this task force made some seventy-nine recommendations. Following this, there were three federal government departments that initiated programs by designating funds available for counseling and long-term work with crime victims. They started funding self-help support groups across Canada. Manitoba was one of the leading provinces.

The year Candace was murdered, they were starting to fund police victim services and support groups with almost $30,000 to get started. It helped defray the expenses of promotional material, rent, and hiring facilitators.

Except that – judging from the president's voice – there was still something missing. The concept of justice was now elusive. The idea of forgiveness was offensive.

For every action there is a reaction, they say. A desperate, new undertow developed that tried to move justice in a different direction – an alternative.

That's when the movement, Restorative Justice, gained momentum. This new movement was presenting itself as an alternative to the traditional justice system.

I don't think it is a coincidence that this new way of approaching justice emerged during the same period that the abolition of capital punishment was being discussed. The simple solutions were gone. Those who were working within the system were now also exploring new ways to do justice.

If punishment – the old way of doing justice – was proving to be ineffective and costly, what were the other, alternative ways to deal with the harm of murder?

Restorative Justice was popularly defined as an alternative to justice. Since crime causes harm, true justice should focus on repairing that harm. And the people most affected by the crime should be able to participate in its resolution.

The Mennonites had a history with this. They had been working at this in their communities for a long time ever since their founder, Menno Simons, a pacifist, had started them on the eternal quest for alternatives to violence. It was in our DNA as a people that had been dealing with counter-cultural ways of doing justice for five centuries.

At the forefront of this movement was a Mennonite story, an initiative that caught the attention of Correctional Service of Canada.

It was called the "Elmira Case." In 1974, two intoxicated teenagers had gone on a destructive rampage damaging numerous properties in the quiet town of Elmira, Ontario. Ordinarily, the prospect of prison lay ahead. But a pair of young probation officers had other ideas. They asked the presiding judge, rather than prison, what if the youths actually met their victims face to face?

They suggested this would allow the youths to apologize to the victims and pay for damages. The judge actually listened to their plea and ordered the teenagers, guilty of vandalism, to make restitution directly to their victims.

The two young men, Mark Yantzi, who was a probation officer and his friend, Dave Worth, a Mennonite Central Committee (MCC) volunteer, were directed by the court to oversee the reconciliation process. More cases soon followed, and the MCC of Ontario's Victim Offender Reconciliation Project (VORP) was formed.

This was the birth story of a movement.

Because of my position as a Mennonite reporter, I had met Dave Worth, the National Director of VORP, shortly after Candace's death at an MCC conference being held in British Columbia. I had to interview him on various occasions after that.

In turn, he knew about our case, and it was very quickly established that even though his work in reconciliation was wonderful – our case, the murder of our daughter, didn't fit into his program. For one thing, I didn't know who the offender was – and besides that, VORP wasn't working with victims of a serious crime such as murder.

20

But that didn't stop me from continuing the conversation with him and the others involved in the movement.

It was the perfect storm. Abolishing the death penalty was forcing victims to choose between frustrated anger – or forgiveness.

Restorative justice programs required a measure of forgiveness.

Except those in the VORP organization were also in communication with the offenders.

I soon realized that, for a parent of a murdered child, there is an almost visceral reaction to convicted offenders as people. The offenders smell of death – an obnoxious scent. Those who kill are from the dark side – to be avoided at all cost.

And those who were in communication with offenders were also from the dark side.

Since I had chosen forgiveness, I knew that I had, to some degree, come to terms with this aversion, distaste, even hate. But those who didn't have that inclination instinctively wanted to eliminate the scent – and those giving off the scent.

David Worth was someone working in this field who seemed to understand both. He understood the offenders. He had their loyalty.

However, he seemed to also understand me – and the group I represented. He was empathic.

And we did have a common concern – a common enemy as it were. It was the justice system. Both communities – offenders and victims – agreed that the justice system was inadequate and needed to be tweaked, if not changed completely.

We all agreed that we wanted to avoid the traditional way of doing justice.

Not only was I reporting on the events that included Restorative Justice, my office was right in the middle of a hub of Mennonite activity. I was surrounded. I was engulfed. I was a Mennonite journalist. It was also about proximity as well.

The paper I worked for, the *Mennonite Reporter*, was an independent, inter-Mennonite paper of news and comment, circulated across Canada and beyond. It was recognized as an active member of The Canadian Church Press (from which it received many awards over the years), Meetinghouse (an association of Mennonite editors), and, for a time, the US-based Associated Church Press.

Not only was I connected in my work, but my office was also on the same floor as many of the other Mennonite organizations in the city. At this time, Winnipeg and the surrounding area had a significant population of cultural Mennonites, enough to consider it the highest in the world.

During this time, a Mennonite businessman, John Schroeder, who owned the Assiniboine Travel Services, and who possessed a particular passion for Mennonite history, created a kind of mini-Mennonite enclave of like-minded businesses and charities. Right next to his office on the same floor was this odd collection of offices: Mennonite Books, Mediation Services, Mennonite Mirror, Manitoba Chamber Orchestra, and the denominational paper that I worked for. Even though we all worked for different organizations, we were colleagues – and we often had informal hallway conversations that were important to me.

The word that tied us together was a cultural understanding of the word "forgiveness." They used it. I used it. They didn't need an explanation, they didn't hold me to it, they simply understood.

Chapter 4
GREENDALE

I looked up. The clouds were hovering closer now – starting to release their moisture. It was coming out as snow. I was relieved.

I needed white. I love white.

The Prairies do snow well. It floats like pure icing sugar – tiny, soft, powdery flecks of snow. It was like a white bridal veil – obscuring my view of the dismal parking lot beneath my window with an intimate cloud of white.

Innocence – purity.

I heard a door open and shut down the hallway. I was in Mennonite land here in this office building. I wondered which Mennonite was passing down the hallway.

The truth of it was, I wasn't only working for a Mennonite paper placed in an enclave of Mennonite organizations, I was born a Mennonite.

I was so Mennonite. I'm sure if I wanted to, I could trace my own DNA to our founder, Menno Simons, who started the movement 500 years ago. I belonged to this nomad tribe who kept moving from country to country.

According to my DNA, my family moved from England to Holland, where they converted to the Mennonite way. Then because of the Mennonites' unpopular Anabaptist stance, they were persecuted – forcing them to flee Holland to Prussia. Targeted there as well, they moved to Russia to settle by the Black Sea. During the Russian Revolution, they were targeted again, and fled to Canada settling in British Columbia in the Fraser Valley – Greendale to be exact, where I grew up.

I was steeped in the Mennonite culture, attending a Mennonite Brethren church every Sunday, prayer meetings on Wednesday and German school Saturday morning. After elementary school, I was bussed to Mennonite Educational Institute (MEI) in Clearbrook. After graduation I travelled to Hepburn, Saskatchewan to attend Bethany Bible Institute, where I met my prairie love of my life, who was also very much a Mennonite. Once married, we were off to Mennonite Brethren Bible College in Winnipeg where my husband trained to be a Mennonite pastor. After our children were born, I took journalism at Red River Community College and then accepted a position as Western Regional Editor of a church denominational paper known as the *Mennonite Reporter*.

I was a pure-blooded Mennonite – living in the Mennonite capital of the world, dedicated to my Mennonite career.

Nothing in my Mennonite roots could have prepared me for being on stage with a notorious criminal. We as a people feared being noticed. We went to great lengths to avoid any confrontation. We shunned evil – and loved our quiet ways. In fact, we were known as the quiet in the land.

However, there was something even back then that had set me on this path…that had led me here. It was the word forgiveness….

My father owned a Shell service station in a rural part of the Fraser Valley known as Greendale.

It was the perfect place to grow up – as good as it is possible to be – a wonderful mix of rural and urban life. We could run from our house over to the garage which was on the same yard to get a chocolate bar from a tiny confectionery then slip into our little white barn, still on the same yard, and watch a newborn calf learn to suck milk from a pail and then back into our house again for a dinner of perogies and farmer sausage.

I was the third daughter born five years after my two older sisters – definitely a rerun. I had no exceptional talents; I was nondescript, shorter than my three beautiful sisters. I was the one that was destined for an undistinguished life. I was invisible.

The only thing I had going for me was my bond with my father – not that he noticed me much but I adored him and followed him around like a little puppy.

Looking back, I realize now that I never bonded with my mother. She was truly a wonderful, caring mother, but who was ill at the time of my birth.

So early on, I spent all of my time in the garage with my father, my babysitter, watching him fix the cars. I loved nothing better than listening and watching the customers talk to my father – who considered him very wise.

Since I was invisible, he didn't mind me being there. I learned that there are advantages to being a spectator of life and loved it. It was almost like having a super power to go into a stealth mode. He seemed to enjoy having an invisible listener to talk to when there were no customers.

When he was busy, my most favorite place was sitting in a huge chestnut tree right beside the station where I could watch him fill gas and serve his customers. I was meant to be in the audience, not on the stage.

I was probably in Grade Three when, as I was swinging on the school swings with three of my cousins, an older boy came by. I heard him say sarcastically, "Isn't it just like the Mennonites to hog the swings!"

Mennonite? He had just referred to me as a Mennonite. I had never even heard the term before. At home, I asked my sister, "What is a Mennonite?"

She paused, took a deep breath, and recited in her big sister tone, "They're a people who wear black bonnets, won't own cars, and only ride in horse-drawn buggies. They don't have electricity in their homes, the women aren't allowed to wear any makeup, and they all live together in a large community. They are known for sewing quilts."

"Are we Mennonites?" I asked cautiously.

"Yes."

"But we don't live like that. We don't sew quilts."

"There are thousands of different kinds. We're more modern, but we're still Mennonites."

I listened to her incredulously. She wasn't making any sense, and she didn't even realize it.

Dad always made sense, so I went directly to him. He was bent over his workbench, fixing a small motor. He explained that, yes, there were many different types of Mennonites, but the one thing they all had in common was that they believed in non-resistance.

"What's that?" I asked.

"We don't believe in going to war." Then he described how he, as a young man, had developed a hernia which made him unfit for the army. He seemed conflicted about it. He talked about a friend of his who had served in the war – and then was ostracized by the Mennonites. He described how society at large frowned on anyone who refused to go to war. Apparently, it had been a no-win situation.

Then he went on to explain that to be a true Mennonite meant more than being a pacifist. It meant believing that peace is part of believing in God. "We take it seriously when the Bible says that you should love your enemies, that when someone hits you on one cheek, you should turn the other." He also said Mennonites were known for their forgiving lifestyle.

Forgiveness!

I saw the nitty-gritty forgiveness lifestyle being modeled.

As we became teenagers, my three sisters, one brother, and I were trained to serve gasoline at the pumps. Because my father trusted everyone in the community, he allowed the customers who came to the pumps for gas to call out "charge it" and drive off without bothering to sign.

However, one day our father told all of us that one particular neighbor was not allowed to "charge it" anymore. I knew immediately why. My father's bookkeeping system was to fill out a bill and file it in a huge, gray account book open for all of us to see. The man owed dad a huge amount of money. I was shocked.

By this time, as an inquisitive teenager, I asked, "Why don't you do something about it? Can't you take him to court to have him settle this?"

My father was horrified. "No. Mennonites don't take people to court. It says in the Bible that, in the church, we are to settle it among ourselves peacefully."

"Then why don't you take him in front of the church? That's in the Bible too."

"Then what would come of it? I would get my money, but how would he feel? How would the church feel?"

"But you're out of a lot of money!"

He just shrugged his shoulders. "He's an honest man. He will pay when he has the money."

Every Sunday, I would watch this financially-delinquent man sitting near the front of the church, and I would wonder how in the world God could tolerate such injustice in his own house.

One evening, I heard my father say to Mom, "That man has more problems than I have. He will pay when he can." The issue of justice becomes obsolete when a bad debt turns into a gift. Dad was no longer wronged; he had given the money away.

Years later, the man eventually paid.

The sociologist quoted in the *Windsor Star* had been right – it was a Mennonite thing. And I was learning that there was a kind of justice that did eventually happen.

I was also learning that forgiveness wasn't meant to be passive.

I'll never forget the day that I came home from school and found a police car parked in our driveway and the officers talking to my father.

My mother explained that the garage had been broken into, and someone had emptied the cash till not only of the money but also dad's rare coin collection.

My father had called the police! He had never called the police for any of the other break-ins!

We were Mennonites – we didn't call in law enforcement. So, with a feeling of righteous indignation and a whole lot of youthful idealism, I wondered out loud at the dinner table that night, how "a people" who claimed to be non-resistant when it came to war, who called themselves pacifists – would call the police when they needed protection at home.

There was dead silence. A kind of weariness passed over my father's eyes – he didn't say anything – he just stared at me.

I stared back defiantly. These weren't just idle musings on my part. This was extremely important to me. I wanted him to be true to his words. I wanted him to be consistent in every detail of his life. I desperately needed him to be consistent.

He started to rationalize – by saying that he hadn't hired the police, he had just called them. That's why we had police, he said. It was their job....

Then I told him quite bluntly that I thought it was wrong "to claim to be a pacifist and then expect other people to do your dirty work."

As you can imagine, the gloves came off at that point, and the discussion became very heated. We got up from the supper table and the discussion spilled over into the entire evening, with each of us aiming well-positioned remarks at the other.

He went into all kinds of Mennonite history – *selbstschutz* and things like that. I pulled out the "Jesus dying on the cross" card. It got nasty – well, as nasty as a good, peace-loving-Mennonite, fighting-over-pacifism discussion can get.

Ironically, in this discussion, I was the one defending pacifism – and he was arguing the right to defend oneself. And yet he was the one who was the "die-hard Mennonite" – or so I thought. I was just playing the devil's advocate.

At the end of the evening, I had gone upstairs to my bedroom quite disillusioned with the hypocrisy of it all and I resolved to strike him off of my "most admired people" list.

I'm sure he went to bed tired beyond reason. Here he was working twelve-hour days solving other people's car problems, dealing with a major personal and public injustice – and then on top of all that having to listen to an upstart teenager who thought she knew it all, and who was irritating at the best of times.

The next morning, still groggy with sleep, I was surprised to find my father at the bottom of the stairs waiting for me.

His countenance was dark. There were significant shadows under his eyes, and I was immediately sorry for my explosion the evening before. I had defied him – and he didn't take defiance lightly.

Seeing him standing there looking so distraught, I knew I had stepped over the line. I was usually more careful with him.

Just as I was about to apologize, he said, "If I claim to be a pacifist, I was wrong yesterday to call the police."

I thought I hadn't heard correctly. Was he really admitting that he was wrong?

Then he said it in a way I could understand. "And you were right. If we as a people claim to be truly non-resistant, I should not have called the police."

Then before I could answer him, he pulled on his work cap and headed for the door.

I ran after him.... "But Dad...."

He just shrugged and waved another apology. "I guess I'm not a pure pacifist," he said as he opened the back door and disappeared.

I ran to the window to watch him walk down the sidewalk to the gas station. Tears were rolling down my cheeks.

He truly was a hero.

I had just won my first war of words.

It was all about words in our family. And it was words that had paved the way for me to be on this notorious stage.

I remember the family gatherings at my grandmother's house. After feasting on a lovely dinner, the adults would close the French doors behind them as they gathered in the living room – the children were not allowed to go inside.

And then they laughed and laughed.

We could hear them outside.

As the evening wore on it seemed to get louder and louder. I was curious. Since I was the littlest, I knew that by rubbing my sleepy eyes, I would be allowed in. Knowing how to be invisible was a distinct advantage at this point because I could act tired and then slip onto my mother's lap – feign sleep on my mother's lap and listen to what they laughed about.

It was all about stories.

My father was an excellent storyteller. Actually, the entire Bergmann side of our family loved stories. They would tell story after story, until the tears ran down Aunt Susie's cheeks. I would fall asleep to the sound of the story.

I was left with this immense yearning to tell stories as they did.

I must have been in Grade Five when a customer who couldn't pay for whatever maintenance was required came to my father's Shell service station and gave him an old manual typewriter. One of those ancient Underwood typewriters, tall, black, and already an antique – even back then. Dad was so excited when he bestowed it on my older sister who had just won a class prize for being a promising storyteller. I just ached to touch it. But she wouldn't let me till she found out that it had no period. With disgust, she carried that heavy thing to the machine shop section of the barn and left it on the workbench.

On one side of our duplex barn was a place for our one cow – on the other side was a workshop – a kind of storage room with windows facing a pigsty that was often inhabited by pink, grunting, easily-excitable pigs.

Without anyone really noticing, I rearranged the workshop, emptied the storage area, and fashioned my first writing studio. I cut out scenery pictures from magazines and tacked them onto the wall so I wouldn't have to look out the windows at the pigsty. Then I claimed that big heavy Underwood, placed it on my own hastily assembled workbench made of boxes and a discarded piece of plywood, and started to type. Who needed a period?

Eventually, the lack of a period was annoying so I placed a broken-off pencil lead in the hole where the period was supposed to be – and it did create a kind of dot. It was set a little high – but it was there – the best I could do.

I found some white paper from somewhere and started to type out my first novel.

I was going to be a novelist – a storyteller.

I practiced and practiced and practiced.

When Candace disappeared and we found the journalists asking us for our story – I was not intimidated by their need for words. It wasn't only their need for story that I was fulfilling. Words and stories were how I processed my own pain, and made sense of it all.

If I were honest with myself, I would have to admit that it was my love of words and my storytelling that had brought me to this stage. But sharing it with a notorious criminal – that was still a stretch.

Chapter 5
SURVIVORS SUPPORT GROUP

I noticed that the wind had picked up and the soft flakes of snow were taking on a new look – almost invisible. The precipitation was turning to rain…. I could hear ice pellets on the office windows.

The drive home would not be pleasant, I thought, as I tried to finish the article that I was working on. But those churning clouds outside, hurling rain and snow at my windows, were unsettling me – strangely. It was as if they were an image of my own churning restlessness of unresolved issues.

I bent over my computer. The sooner I wrote my article – the sooner I could get on the road and beat the rush of sliding cars, but I found myself lost in memories.

Then I remembered that first meeting of the survivors support group for parents of murdered parents.

It was a shock. I expected a group of grieving parents, but they weren't.

They were all headliners.

The murders of our children had put every one of us on the front page of the newspapers.

At that time, we were meeting in a rather unique church, an old converted house that looked like a tiny, white castle on Notre Dame, the perfect setting for us – casual and a little chaotic.

I felt at home immediately. The members' issues were familiar, their words were uninhibited, and I felt accepted.

The group didn't start with the usual time for chitchat. We had serious issues to talk about. We shared encounters with the police. We compared notes about lawyers, judges, and psychologists in the city. It seemed we were connected to all the organizations and agencies in the city but didn't belong to any of them. We could cry one moment and rant the next.

We would usually start the evening with our credo.

We are all surviving victims of murder. Someone we loved very dearly was taken violently from us. We have come here tonight because we believe that by sharing our story, and by listening to others share their stories, we will begin to find meaning in our experience. By giving it words, we will find understanding. By giving it tears, we will find healing.

This is our safe place. We trust each other not to be critical, not to use what we say against us, and not to repeat it outside of these walls.

Here we allow full expression of our grief. We are allowed to use the words we want, to vent, to cry, to laugh, to hug, or to sit quietly.

(Yes, swearing was allowed – if not encouraged!)

There is no pain too big or small, that we cannot share.

We will give each other equal time. We will go around our circle of sharing and each person will have a couple of minutes of uninterrupted time to say whatever lies in their hearts.

During our discussions, we can ask questions, sympathize, share our own stories, but cannot interpret someone else's story for them. Our stories are our own. We cannot presume to know what is best for someone else.

Remembering always – we are among friends. We are with people who understand, who have been there, who have felt the same pain, the same anger, the same despair. It is our like experience that bonds us, and it is our sharing that will make us stronger – because we are survivors.

We had a bond. We had one thing in common. We had been leading ordinary lives when suddenly our child was murdered, and we were thrown into a situation completely foreign to us, which had its own emotions, its own vocabulary and its own customs. We had no background, no understanding, and no grid. It was hard to find anyone with answers – no one understood us. It seemed to be uncharted territory not only for us but for everyone around us.

We all had trauma clouds attached to our hearts.

At my first meeting, the president explained that I was joining because I was a parent of a murdered child and that, even though I was known for my forgiveness stance, I would not promote forgiveness in any way.

Just the hint of the word sent their personal formation of clouds into a thunderous rage. I could see it happening in front of me as they began to share their stories of well-meaning friends telling them to "just forgive." As they talked, the clouds were getting darker, growing and starting to writhe – torturing them.

I tried to explain to them that I was in this group for my own healing – not to fight with their clouds. I explained that I, too, thought it offensive when churches and friends expected us to "just forgive" – not having any idea of how difficult it was. In fact, that's why I was joining the group. I had realized that I needed help.

Everyone relaxed after that.

I noticed that the clouds, though still hovering, were watching me with hooded eyes. It seems I could distract them with simple integrity. They were disarmed by my curiosity – my vulnerability. But they were watching….

We continued with the program.

I remember the first circle question was: Do you feel you are going crazy?

Yes. They all agreed. It felt as if they were going crazy.

It was wonderful to admit to the craziness of our world.

Then we went around the circle again.

The woman to my right began. "When the police appeared at the door, I didn't want to let them in because I thought as long as they stayed out there, it was going to be alright. It was when they came inside the door…. I knew they always brought bad news. But the officer kept saying, 'We need to come in and talk to you.'

"Finally, I let them in. It's like your mind already knows – and wants to stall.

"When they told me my son had been killed, I couldn't breathe. I kept saying, 'Are you sure?' And he kept saying, 'Yes.'

"I was like the Rock of Gibraltar when people were there. But when they left, I would just fall apart. I just didn't care about anything. If the beds weren't made for three weeks, I didn't care. I really didn't care if I lived or died.

"The first week, I picked up the phone and literally dialed my son's number hoping when it rang that he would answer – but he didn't. He never answered his phone…again."

The tears were flowing.

And then the woman next to her began telling her story.

Sometimes the stories flowed easily – beautifully. Sometimes the storytellers were lost in their own script looking for a way into their next paragraph – as if the words were freefalling. Sometimes there were long silences as they struggled to control their feelings. The next time the words might flow in a swift torrent of churning emotions. It was all good. We were safe in our no-judgment zone.

What made this group especially interesting to me was how articulate people were when it came to describing the "violation" of our lives. Most of them had led rather conventional lives before the event. There was nothing that could have prepared them for their loss and the murder….

We were all struggling with what we called the "aftermath of murder."

At least that is what we called it in our group – really it was that vicious presence that haunted our every move.

I had different names for it.

Shortly after that first meeting, the president asked if I would join the board; they needed help in negotiating this new initiative. And then a few months after I had joined, the president and his wife resigned from the board. I was devastated.

At the time I was working full time. My two other children were now asking questions and needing help. Cliff was struggling. Yet there was no one else to take the leadership. By this time, the program had already proved itself to the members, so we couldn't just let it die.

Reluctantly, I took on the role of "acting president." Knowing I needed help as much as the others, I decided to invite different speakers to our group meetings – each with different psychological expertise – to come and talk to our survivors support group about "issues," so we would begin to understand this terrifying new beast in our lives.

After a grief counselor spoke, we learned that it was "complicated grief." But that wasn't enough. There was more.

After a priest came to speak, we learned to call it the dark night of the soul, a period of utter spiritual desolation, disconnection, and emptiness in which one feels totally separated from the Divine.

Through the speakers, we found different names for it – depression, social anxiety, fragmentation.

When one of our members told me of an American friend, a Vietnam War veteran, that was passing through Winnipeg to visit her, we asked her if she might invite him to come to our meeting and talk to us about his experiences.

It was most enlightening. We learned first-hand that the Vietnam War lasted from 1964 to1973 – the longest war in American history. Unlike other wars, the veterans came back from Vietnam by themselves, rather than together with their units or companies, so there was no preparation for their return. They were fragmented. So it took nearly twenty years after the end of the war for the country to learn to deal with these veterans that came home in a traumatized state – once referred to as "shell shock."

He described Post Traumatic Stress Disorder – something that he was struggling with. We had never heard of it. He wondered vaguely if we felt it might apply to us.

After his explanation, we resonated with him immediately. I went out and bought the book *Trauma and Recovery* by Judith Herman, which was hailed as a ground-breaking work at that time. In the book, Herman drew on her own cutting-edge research of combat veterans and victims of political terror and domestic violence to show the parallels.

We drew our own parallels. Except we resisted being told that we had a disorder. For us, it was just a normal reaction to an abnormal event.

It became our routine program – inviting speakers. And after each speaker's presentation, we would call a coffee break, guide the speaker out the door – then settle down again and discuss the topic as it related to our group. We rearranged these new findings into a language more to our liking and then went around the circle to share our stories that applied to the subject of the evening.

I watched, observed, and even documented every discovery, every move.

In 1991 our survivors support group was awarded $136,000 from the Manitoba government – we could finally do more. We hired an executive director.

After one of our meetings, the speaker told me that she had never quite experienced a group like ours before. It seemed more intense – more...something.... She didn't seem to have the words for it.

I knew she had sensed the presence of the trauma clouds – always circling, always threatening.

It wasn't until I was invited to attend a Compassionate Friends support meeting that I realized the difference between grieving the natural death of a child and that of a murdered child. In a natural death due to accident or illness, there was no black cloud inside or outside. Those parents were dealing with enormous grief, complicated grief – but with none of the issues of a serious crime.

Because of this, they would clutch the pictures of their children in their hands and talk endlessly about their child – and cry and cry. They cried for themselves and for each other. It was such a healthy process.

When I went back to our group, I noticed that every time we shared our stories, we rarely talked about our children. We were instead obsessed with the murderer.

I remember one evening especially when we were stuck in an endless discussion about whether we should use the murderer's given name. Somehow, we could never use it. We called the person "he" or even "it." We wondered if we should use a respectable justice label, such as offender – or perhaps even perpetrator. Or should we call them what our hearts wanted to call them – killers, murderers – or even worse.

As we discussed this, I noticed the black clouds on the edge of the room were growing at twice the rate of those within. I had always thought that the clouds on the outskirts were extensions of the personal clouds but they weren't.

They seemed to be triggered by our talk about the offenders. I began to understand that this cloud wasn't only about our trauma – but was bonded with that of the offender.

I was surprised that I, too, was caught up in this offender cloud. I didn't even know who had murdered my daughter, yet I found myself stalked by that imaginary presence.

"I will forgive," I said repeatedly, which seemed to keep the haunting clouds at bay at least for me for the moment. But in this room of victims the dark clouds had full reign. They were growing – slithering back and forth.

This wasn't good because the clouds were unconsciously distracting everyone from grieving.

So we instituted a new policy. We were to bring pictures of our children to the meetings. We began to enforce a kind of memorial at the end of each evening at which time we would concentrate on our children.

We would cry and cry and cry some more.

As I had hoped, the vulnerability of our tears did shrink the threatening, black clouds somewhat. It definitely diminished the growl.

Chapter 6
FACE TO FACE

I couldn't write. I finally got up, made myself a cup of coffee and continued staring out the window.

Those clouds were still churning outside – my thoughts were still churning inside me.

Now we were back to snow. Back to the little flecks of snow that couldn't seem to land. They were swirling around in the wind, too light to land.

Odd weather.

This was called blinding snow, a new kind of danger for the ride home. Slowly – we would be crawling home – slowly, impatiently.

I set the coffee mug down. But the computer monitor remained blank.

Then the memories took over again.

I remembered the day there was a light tap on the door of my office.

I didn't have a lot of visitors coming to my little office in the furthest corner of the huge office building on Portage Avenue.

"Come in," I said uncertainly, wondering who it would be.

It was a man from the office next door.

"May I sit?" he asked.

"Yes," I nodded – returning to my desk.

"As you might know, we are starting a new program…." he said, settling uneasily in the chair opposite my desk. "It's called Face to Face."

I had wondered when he would come – the newly appointed director of this new restorative justice movement, Jake Letkemen.

"You might not fit the criteria of our program, because you don't know the perpetrator – but since you are the president of Family Survivors of Homicide, I was wondering if your members might be interested in our program."

By this time, I had been with the survivors support group for three years. It had grown to about 130 members.

He continued.

"Right now, we don't have the right coordinators in place. We are working with a group out of Stony Mountain Institution called Justice Program, but they haven't received permission.... I was wondering if we might introduce it slowly – perhaps by just writing letters at first."

"Letters?"

He nodded.

He was watching me closely. "Would you like to participate in a kind of pen pal program?"

"What would that look like?" I asked. "Would we find the inmates and then match them to their victims?" That didn't sound safe.

"No – just an exchange of letters between random lifers and members of your group. Open letters – just to get started."

That sounded safer.

"I'll think about it," I said.

He nodded and left.

My office was right next to Mediation Services, which had been established in 1979 in response to a concern both for people victimized by crime and for the high number of people being incarcerated in Canada. By 1983 the justice system was already referring selected pre-trial court cases to mediation.

In their work of mediation, they were moving more and more into victim and offender services. Face to Face was their newest initiative.

One couldn't be closer – more connected to it all – than I was.

Next group meeting, I asked the members whether they would consider being pen pals with men on the inside.

They said, "No!" – shocked that I would even ask.

Their black clouds were eyeing mine.

Jake came back a few days later for my answer.

I said no – they did not want to correspond.

He seemed disappointed and then shared with me the work of Mark Umbreit, a consultant for the National Victim Offender Reconciliation Resource Center in the United States.

I had read about some of his work in his newsletter. Whereas Jake was suggesting only writing letters, Umbreit was setting up actual meetings between victims and offenders.

He stated, "Mediation of victim/offender conflict is not a panacea, nor is it an option for all victims. Yet, there are few other programs within the criminal justice process that so directly hold the offender personally accountable to their victims."

His program was designed mainly for non-violent property offenses of theft and burglary. However, a program in Oklahoma had found that the victim/offender mediation processes were effective with violent offenses as well, such as survivors of negligent homicide victims, victims of armed robbery and some assaults.

Umbreit had written, "When we victim advocates impose programs on vulnerable victims or make choices for them, we come dangerously close to the sort of re-victimization we work to avoid in the first place."

He also said that victim advocates view the victim/offender mediation skeptically…. He then asserted that even though this might not make for a complete victim service agency, it was, however, a viable part of solid, comprehensive victim assistance programs. Victims deserve the option of choosing mediation, just as they deserve the option of choosing to participate in counseling.

I was skeptical both as a victim and as an advocate.

"Mediation?" I asked. "If it's homicide, what is there to talk about, reconcile or agree about?"

Letkemen agreed.

"I recognize that there is something that might bring about more offender empathy – but what is there in it for the victim?" It wasn't about reconciliation he assured me. "It is just about meeting them – and listening to each other's stories."

Apparently, "the victims," who engaged in these meetings, had the rare opportunity to let the criminals know how the crime affected them.

Umbreit had written, "Many wanted to tell the perpetrators things such as: What you did not only hurt me, it brutalized my children and my husband. Offenders learn the real impact of their behavior. They can take direct responsibility for what they did by attempting to make amends to the person they violated." I realized why the Criminal Justice System might be open to this. There were benefits for the criminals – a chance at change – even rehabilitation.

For our group? There was no such benefit. These were victims of violent crime. Period. All the literature, in fact, pointed out that it wasn't being tried with homicide victims of murder – criminal negligence perhaps – but not killers.

Letkemen came to talk to me a few times, and I would listen but pull back. It just wouldn't fit.

Yet I couldn't let it go. By this time, observing the group, I had isolated a "victim-offender trauma bond" as one of the issues facing victims in our group discussion.

Crime is about broken relationships. The more violent the crime, the more difficult it is to re-establish a trust relationship so offenders and victims are bonded together in an unfinished justice agenda. Some of these unresolved issues are: the need for information, the need for protection, prevention and the validation of the feelings of rage, guilt, and fear.

I wrote to someone at the time:

One of the biggest surprises after the murder of my own daughter was the strong mixed feelings I had towards the person who had taken her life. I expected the anger and resentment, but what I didn't expect was the closeness. It's almost as if this person is now part of our lives. And in our case, since I don't know the identity of this person, and still don't know, it was difficult to define exactly what this meant or how to understand it.

I am only aware that suddenly I have a "relationship" with this faceless person. I was relieved to discover that my husband felt the same way – that this act of violence had tied us all together.

My question: What do we do with this relationship? How do we understand it? How do we keep it in perspective?

The reality is that victims are connected to the offender in an unfinished justice-making process. I had seen it in a million different ways. They were obsessed with the whereabouts of the offender. They needed to know everything about this person, in order to feel safe again. I began to realize that if they didn't deal with this trauma bond, they would never get control of their lives again.

It was simple. They needed to deal with their black cloud.

Finally, I decided that, even though an actual meeting was out of the question, I would write my own letter – that's all that Letkemen had been asking in the first place.

I told him I would entertain a letter – no promises.

In a very short time, the first inmate letter came in the mail from Curtis. It was eleven pages of legal-size paper – typed.

I have been in Stony Mountain Institution since I was convicted of Second-Degree Murder…. I am a lifer. A "lifer" is a person doing a life sentence, I understand the victim has no time off from his death, or we would have seen him or her already. Believe me, I wish many times to be dead with the dead, for they may be more human and forgiving….

He went into detail about his sentence.

It is a violent thought that I could or may be "forgiven" for the crime, only when I die.

Murder is a continuous punishment for the living, no compassion, or room for any healing, the offenders and survivors forever separated.

I am buried alive inside a coffin made of steel and concrete with many others, all screaming and yelling to get out. But, no one answers the call for help, justice has been done. Left alone with no satisfaction of healing. Yet, I breathe and try to survive even though I have been reduced to sub-human. I struggle to prove I am still human, that can care and be cared for. I try to survive and do something for our hurts to get on with our personal lives. I carry and wave the banner of love that says we are human. Yes, we make mistakes, and there will always be mistakes, as many as there are correct, constructive and positive ones. Wrong and rights are what we make them be.

Then he wrote. *Even on the entrance into prison, the murderer is treated as non-existent. He is treated as if he killed thousands of people, rated right along with Hitler and Khan, or any mass killer. It is tough living life when people treat you "as not being alive at all." To survive, one has to pick up animal instincts of non-caring and forgetting the everyday punishment.... There is never a justification for murder nor is there to forever withhold forgiveness and healing.*

It was that last sentence that shook me the most!

I couldn't read any further. The growling of the shadow cloud was distracting. I tried many times – I just couldn't. I didn't even want to touch the letter. I carried the letter with the tips of my fingers and kept it secure in an envelope. I didn't want it to touch anything.

It was a letter, pleading for empathy – and I had none.

Now I needed support, so I personally approached one of the members of the group to see if they would consider at least reading the letter for me and giving me their response.

They talked to someone else – and finally, there were four of them who would read it – but they wanted to do it together. One of the members even offered his home as a place to meet.

So, I took it to them.

Since I couldn't read it, I asked if someone would read it aloud for us.

We really tried to get through it. Each one would start reading – and then stop – and pass it on.

It was as if the black presence of the trauma cloud had taken hold of us all.

We tried reading.

Parts of the letter were a lament, some of it was advocacy, some of it was teachings on forgiveness complete with diagrams…. Some of it was asking – some of it was preaching – some of it was blaming.

We couldn't get through it without handing it to someone – unfinished.

After every few sentences, we would burst into rants of anger or simple unbelief at what he was saying.

I don't think we ever got through the entire letter.

Finally, exhausted, at the end of the evening, I dared to ask the question, "Should we meet with them?"

"No," they said.

"Are you sure?"

They paused, incredulous that I couldn't get it. "Definitively not!"

Then, as a group, we came up with twenty-seven points of contention….

Our contentions: Does he have the right to tell us what to do? Is he trying to lead the way? Does he find healing in writing this letter? Do we experience the same healing as we read it?

How dare he insinuate that if survivors do not forgive, they are the same as a killer?

No, we would not meet.

"OK, we won't deal with this inmate," I concluded. "But what about the Face to Face program – what if it is a good program?" I asked the group.

They were unimpressed. "If you are interested, you can research the program," they said. "You handle them. But we want nothing to do with it."

I went home that night, deciding that it wasn't worth it. I didn't even want to engage in the letter writing.

I wasn't about to welcome more blackness – more clouds – more of those shapeshifting presences – into my life.

Chapter 7
UNDERTOW

My coffee was gone. My first draft incoherent. I looked out my window. I was mesmerized with those clouds hovering, not moving. It wasn't raining or snowing. Silent. They were just outside there peering in at me.

But the minute I started watching them, they noticed me and started to move again...churning.

Clouds! Those very first shapeshifting clouds had been following me all these years. Sometimes bringing snow, the next time sleet, but mainly they just churned around me. Sometimes snarling, sometimes flicking a forked tongue...sometimes just grinning.

I had learned to keep them at bay with that one word.... But that word wasn't available to me today – I wasn't forgiving.

That's why they were smiling.

They weren't smiling the day Marie and I uncovered our shared secret.

It was after a support meeting that she lingered, as I was gathering up the coffee mugs and washing them in the tiny sink in the church kitchen. "I met with him," she said quietly.

I spun around. "You what?"

She smiled as she grabbed a tea towel.

We quickly looked around – everyone had left for the evening.

"How did you do it?"

Her eyes were twinkling.

Marie had joined our group shortly after I had joined the board of directors of the survivors support group. Our president at the time felt that it was the role of this new organization to connect with each newly-victimized family of homicide in Winnipeg – much like the late-night visitor who had come to our house.

So early one evening, he had called me to say that a child – an eight-year-old child – had been killed in a runaway, stolen vehicle incident. The mother was in distress. He had just talked to her over the telephone and said that she would like to meet with a member of the group. Would I be able to see her? He thought I would be the perfect person to introduce her to the group.

After my children were in bed, I dutifully set out into the night, only to encounter an unexpected white-out storm.

I found myself crawling along Lagimodiere Boulevard to a Tim Hortons in the St. Vital Mall area to meet Marie for a late-night coffee. I was amazed to find her there – waiting for me.

Noticing the beginning of the storm, she had tried to call it off but hadn't been able to reach me. When I arrived, she was so impressed with my dedication to the cause – or my stupidity. It was easy to engage with her. We had a wonderful conversation. Then she had told me her story.

She had driven to the Dakota Shopping Centre IGA, to pick up something for lunch after church when a sixteen-year-old boy, who had escaped from a youth center almost three months earlier, noticed her car and attempted to steal it. In the ensuing scuffle with her two sons, one of her sons had jumped out of the car, and the thief, in his frantic effort to get away, had run over her boy – who later died in the hospital.

The youth had also struck two other cars and led the police on a car chase that reached speeds of one hundred kilometers per hour, racing through thirteen stop signs and one red light before stopping.

Marie had been thrust not only into a world of grief but also into the Criminal Justice System – another culture shock.

After our visit at the coffee shop, she had joined the group.

Her joining allowed me to watch first-hand her encounter with all the issues of homicide victimization.

The first was guilt.

Marie, who was working in a bank at the time her son was killed, suddenly started complaining that she was forgetting to lock things down. This was becoming a big problem in a bank where security was important.

"I can't lock things...." she kept repeating, in absolute bewilderment.

Then one evening, we noticed that on her way to her car in the parking lot, she had dropped her car keys twice. As we were saying our good-byes, I noticed the way she dangled them in her fingertips as if they were somehow dangerous to the touch.

It dawned on us. She hadn't locked the door of the car. Was she unconsciously connecting keys with the hijacking of her car? Guilt. She was suffering from guilt.

Right there in the parking lot, we named it. She broke into tears. Marie rarely cried. We put our arms around her and cried with her. "Oh, Marie – as mothers, the guilt is the worst." And we just cried and cried as we all remembered ours. "We love you...."

Amazingly, after that, she had no trouble with keys. Naming it had solved it – well, together with our hugs.

Then the trial – two years later – came and went. She changed.

When the Judge had handed out a sentence of three years in jail for killing her son, she had told the press angrily, "The laws in Canada and the facilities are not adequate to deal with juvenile offenders these days. I think it's unrealistic he has to spend three years.... Our lives were ruined, and he gets three years?"

Her eyes were steely green. "It's just a joke. Why is there a court at all? It's just a waste of time.... I thought people were punished."

She said it over and over again in our group meeting.... As was expected. We were all familiar with the anger she was expressing.

We had all come to accept the presence of her dramatic and very angry, fierce, dark cloud.

I once asked the members about their "revenge fantasies." My fantasy of shooting the killer seemed tame in comparison to the fantasies of the others.

Now, two years after our first conversation in the donut coffee shop, we were still meeting – in our small, homey church on Notre Dame.

"You did what?" I asked again – not sure if I was hearing correctly.

"I met with him."

"How? Who? What happened? And most importantly – why?"

"Why?" She smiled.

We sat down. It was dark outside. We should have been going home, but this was important.

She began to talk. "There has been a part of me after seeing him in court that was intrigued with him. I couldn't believe that the juvenile sitting in court looked so much like my son who had been killed. He was a very good-looking fellow with dark curly hair and a nice, quiet personality. I just had this feeling that, number one, I wanted to see him, and that, number two, it would help me to deal with it. I've always been keenly aware of the danger of bitterness after a random act of violence."

She smiled – "Remember, I was brought up in a country that wasn't very forgiving at all. Ireland was dominated by England for 800 years, and England did absolutely horrendous things to Ireland. They caused famines and put our people into slavery. Our whole history is one disaster after another. And I've found that my people who harbored these bitter feelings about things…. Their lives to me were ruined."

Ironically, the violence she tried to escape in Ireland had reared its ugly head here in Canada.

Apparently, her parish priest who was also chaplain at the Youth Centre where the juvenile was kept, went to visit the juvenile. He then had approached Marie and asked if she would like to meet with the juvenile – as a help to deal with her anger.

It had taken time to arrange the meeting.

When they did meet, Marie said she was surprised at the youth's eager anticipation of the meeting. He confessed he had been waiting for weeks and said the guards had even let him cut his hair and get new shoes for the visit. Marie was the only visitor he had in the year and a half he had been there.

He had been nervous.

"At the time I was carrying a big purse," Marie said with a laugh, "and he told me later that he was convinced that I had a gun in my purse. His friends there said that there was only one reason for me to come, and that was to shoot him."

They had talked for two hours during the visit, and she still can't be sure of all that was said – only at the end. "I told him that I had forgiven him for what he had done because it was very important for me to get on with my life and not to feel that there was somebody out there that I was afraid to meet. I said I didn't wish him bad luck. I just wished that he would never cause anybody else any trauma like he had caused us. This was my wish that I would forgive him if he could get on with his life and try to do something with it."

I could see the shadow of the trauma cloud leave her face as she spoke.

I was shocked. "You believe in forgiveness?"

She nodded. "Forgiveness is something that makes you feel better. It really has little to do with the other person at all. It allows you to get on with life."

We stared at each other.

Since she had brought up the word, I felt I could share my story of forgiveness with her. We were both on the same page.

Even though we appreciated the group's trauma around the word, we both felt that they were stuck and would benefit from embracing some of the forgiveness processes that both of us had experienced.

Then I must have asked her a million questions about her emotional processes. Had she gone into the room expecting to forgive him?

No.

What had moved her to forgive?

Just seeing him vulnerable.

And on and on it went.

After, we both agreed – it must have been the power of meeting – the face to face encounter in a safe setting that had moved her from her anger to compassion.

Forgiveness might start with a decision to do things differently – as we had – but it also entailed a process.

She had proven it – to confront the fear – the negativity – to learn about it. She had not walked away, but she had truly embraced it all.

If she was right – our murderers were our greatest teachers.

We started to scheme. Perhaps giving the others in the survivors support group the choice of entering into prison – their greatest fear – would be a way of moving them into having new discussions and not just recycling the old.

Perhaps we needed to revisit the Curtis letter – he was our only safe contact.

Perhaps it would lead to the resolution the group and I were looking for.

All of a sudden, I wanted to meet Curtis – in person. What harm was there in that?

He had invited us – me. "Let us meet, talk, and heal under the banner of peace."

I reconnected with the Face to Face program and was invited to the penitentiary to talk with the organizers of the Justice Program and meet with the inmates on the committee.

I remember driving up to the Stony Mountain Institution and being ushered into the conference room – all the time wondering if my trauma cloud would react to this setting, but it didn't. Apparently, there was no need for trauma. I was just participating in a preliminary organizational meeting.

It wasn't until I was introduced to Curtis, the author of the eleven-page letter, that I paused – suddenly aware of all that was at stake. He was a murderer.

And yet he wasn't. He was tall, a well-dressed man with a distinct twinkle in his eyes. Yes – a twinkle. That twinkle put me at ease immediately. It was as if he too saw the humor of it all. I also think I recognized the writer in him – as he did in me. He had realized the power of words to process the rage inside – and hence the letter.

After that it was all business. We mainly discussed the dynamics of meeting and what could be accomplished by all the parties involved.

They were motivated. The inmates wanted to meet the victim group – probably as part of their restorative justice rehabilitation program. The Justice Program committee wanted it to be a learning experience with structured workshop-type discussions, and I just wanted to challenge our members to face their biggest fear in a safe way.

I met with them twice, and during each of these meetings, I wasn't overly bothered by the cloud. I was an organizer going into prison to set up a program.

After the two meetings in prison and doing the research, I approached the survivors support group one more time. "Would you want to meet with a group of inmates in prison?"

"What are they like?" they asked.

I smiled. I knew I would have to do a bit of a sales job. It was like entering another world, I explained. I appealed to their sense of adventure – describing it as an exotic world.

Finally, they agreed.

It was almost a year after receiving Curtis' letter that we responded to the invitation to meet and made our way to Stony Mountain Institution. No matter how much I tried to shift the date, we couldn't make it work for Marie. With her busy schedule, she just did not have the time to come with us. I was on my own.

But there were two other group members who were willing to go with me.

Chapter 8
KINGPIN

I would never forget that meeting. I stood up and went to the window. Those clouds! Staring – remembering with me.

We had set the date – March 13, 1992.

At the security gate of the penitentiary, we met with the Justice Program organizers. Then we locked our purses and wallets away, and walked down a long corridor that twisted and turned just enough to lose our entire orientation. We landed up in a gymnasium that had been carefully set up according to the diagrams we had exchanged.

We had planned for this well. They had sent their agenda; I had sent ours – and we blended the two.

As we were entering, someone told us that it was going to be well attended. In fact, even the "kingpin" – the most important inmate in the organization – was going to attend. When we asked what constituted a kingpin, they said, "Oh – he is the one who has killed the most people in prison. He killed two."

The scene was set. There was a long head table in the front with glasses of water. A huge picture was hanging on the wall behind us – a winter scene of a riverbank – ironically, a picture of serenity.

By the time we were ready to start, there were one hundred inmates in the room. Even though they looked very ordinary, we knew that – as a medium/maximum federal institution – there were inmates convicted of serious crimes in the room. And there were killers in the room.

We began – introductions of us, our program – and then into our stories. I was the one to start with my story – almost as an icebreaker. It was to be a simple version – basic facts.

Suddenly there was movement in the room – I had obviously triggered them and everyone was getting up to get coffee. The president suggested that we take a break. He suggested that we go into a discussion because of the emotional response to my story.

When we came back, some men expressed a huge appreciation for my courage.

Then I asked our next storyteller to tell his story. Ronald got up – and he was a changed man. In the survivors support group, he had always presented himself as a very conservative, soft-spoken, gracious man – with a bit of a chuckle – but now he was changed. He preached hellfire and brimstone – not literally – but that's how it felt. His anger was palpable.

His black cloud was one snarling mess.

After his story, the first question from the audience was whether we believed in capital punishment. We avoided answering this… sensing that it was a challenge to us.

We broke again for coffee. They needed it. The air was so tense.

During this break, our next speaker, Emily, told me that she wasn't going to tell her story. I was surprised – she was usually so vocal. I was disappointed. She had this wonderfully deep voice – and colorful language – that would connect with this group – but I had no intention of putting her on the spot.

So, we opened up the next segment with a question and answer floor discussion.

The kingpin – who had been pointed out to us – had started the evening by sitting in the back of the gym. Then he had moved to the middle during the second segment. Now, during our third session, he was even closer. It was as if he was inching forward….

The men, responding to Ronald's story, were filled with gratitude for his courage. They seemed to like his honesty and colorful language.

But then an inmate stood up. It was actually Curtis. Not the Curtis I met in the prior meetings – gracious and respectful with that twinkle in his eye – but the Curtis in the letter, opinionated and defensive. "All of you victims appear to me as if you are monkeys carrying the dead on your backs."

The room went very quiet.

Apparently, this is what Japanese macaque monkeys do. A study reports that mothers sometimes persist in carrying infant corpses until they are covered with flies and completely decayed. "Occasionally, a corpse may be carried until it is mummified."

This was not a pretty image.

He had dared to stir up all the clouds in the gymnasium, inmates' and victims'.

Suddenly there were black clouds in the middle of the room – sizing each other up – ready to engage in a fierce fight. They were growling, baring their teeth – circling.

Emily suddenly stood up. She seemed to grow in size. "I don't care what we look like to you – but I will never ever forgive the person who killed my son."

Her anger was frightening. The whole room was electrified.

My heart stopped. There were one hundred of them, six of us – I was worried.

I was the one responsible for this meeting. If it exploded, I would never forgive myself. That's when I noticed that we didn't have any correctional officers in the room. The organizers that were in the room weren't the type that could have handled a prison revolt.

No one moved. You could have cut the tension with a knife – literally.

And then the kingpin, Gerry – who had moved up to the front – stood up.

"I can't forgive either," he said.

He turned to the crowd of inmates. "Face it – that's why we are all in here. It's because we can't forgive."

There it was – the word forgiveness.

The black clouds kind of dissipated. Not entirely. I don't think they ever leave a prison institution completely – but they were definitely confused – in chaos – a fog hovering above us near the ceiling.

Then Emily was ready to tell her story.

She told it with gusto and the men loved her – identified with her.

In the end, we broke into discussion groups again. Out of the corner of my eye – I saw Ronald walk over to the kingpin – and shake his hand.

There was something magical about that evening that didn't just go away. Something indescribable had happened to all of us and had changed us.

I watched closely to see how the "handshake" had affected Ronald. He wasn't as angry – he seemed intrigued with it as well.

Forgiveness did really have the power to control that which seemed uncontrollable. The angry clouds never did find their way back down…. They were held – suspended in the air.

It was 10:00 p.m. exactly, lockdown time, when the room emptied and we were walked back to the front to gather our coats, purses and wallets.

Snow had fallen during the three-hour visit, and we had to brush our cars off. We gathered at a coffee shop on McPhillips Avenue to debrief – the six of us around two tables.

We were amazed at the openness. We were amazed at how we had appreciated the kingpin. It was pointed out that the swearing had been minimal by the prison population. Except for Ronald who had upped his blue language. We laughed.

We went through it all again, then suddenly we were weary. The adrenaline was gone.

The evening had boiled down to the one word – forgiveness – which I had not been allowed to voice – and still couldn't.

Apparently, it didn't matter what the discussion was – for forgiveness or against it – the power of meeting face to face and telling stories was powerful.

Breaking down the walls – no matter how – was the key. Vulnerability on both sides. There seemed to be a power – a social connection that happens when two people dare to share their lives….

We monitored the members carefully after that.

We were surprised how the stories of the two storytellers affected the other members and even gave them new thoughts, new insights. They, too, became less stuck.

We were surprised at the difference in Ronald. He had moved from being a very brittle, hostile man to someone that could laugh more easily. He didn't recycle his revenge fantasies as often.

When debriefing with the director of Mediation Services, she said, "It is all about dialogue…and storytelling."

People affected by crime want to talk about it, and they often want to talk about it with others who were involved – and it didn't much matter who they were – just anyone halfway knowledgeable about the issues.

That meeting changed something for me.

Forgiveness had been freed – somewhat….

As word got out, organizations were asking me to tell my story. Following one of these talks, a member of Tyndale Publishers who had been in the audience approached me and invited me to send my manuscript to him. It was published in 1991 entitled, *Have you seen Candace?*

Then I met the new national MCC Director of Victim and Offender Ministries, Wayne Northey.

"We're having a conference – would you be able to come?" he asked.

I hesitated.

"Right now, we are interested in victims – we need to hear from victims and why it is so difficult for them to move on. Why are they stuck?"

"Stuck!" It was good to learn that I wasn't the only one looking for an answer to that question.

"I'd love to," I said, almost unable to contain myself. "I am starting to compile a list of issues." Soon after, I received a formal invitation and was flown to Mount Allison University, an undergraduate liberal arts and science university located in Sackville, New Brunswick, where Wayne introduced me to Pierre Allard.

I didn't know why he was so important at the time, but by the deference shown to him – the glowing words used to describe him and his charismatic way – I knew I had met a giant in the restorative justice movement. Dr. Pierre Allard was a Correctional Service of Canada (CSC) chaplain, co-founder of Community Chaplaincy and Assistant Commissioner, Community Engagement Sector, who had worked tirelessly for a more compassionate approach to corrections and for more community involvement.

He defined Restorative Justice as an approach to justice that focuses on repairing the harm caused by crime while holding the offender responsible for his or her actions, by providing an opportunity for the parties directly affected by a crime – victim(s), offender and community – to identify and address their needs in the aftermath of a crime, and seek a resolution that affords healing, reparation, and reintegration, and prevents future harm.

Another leader and developer of restorative justice as a concept was Howard Zehr. His book *Changing Lenses: A New Focus for Crime and Justice* is considered a classic in the field. He defined Restorative Justice as "…a process to involve, to the extent possible, those who have a stake in a specific offense and to collectively identify and address harms, needs, and obligations, to heal and put things as right as possible."

These were the two heroes of the movement whom I admired. I could embrace their definitions as an ideal that I could work towards.

Preparing for this event, I was tempted to work on my power point presentation – organize, decorate, and type in everything perfectly. Then I thought better of it. It was a draft idea of mine still in the making. I had collected seven points – and that's all I would present.

I needed to be authentic.

So instead of preparing a professional power point, I just printed the seven statements out onto a transparency – the way one would draft notes.

I had them projected on the screen behind.

Naming it. It is essential that the crime or issue be named for what it is – murder, rape, assault. Until the crime is acknowledged, it can't be healed.

Stopping it.

Telling the story and expressing emotions.

Validation and re-establishing a social connection.

Researching.

Preventing.

Establishing blame.

I told them that for victims to heal, they need to be in a safe environment with people they trust. These elements are fluid. They can be repeated and can also happen at the same time.

With each point, I elaborated. I told them how hard it was to even identify the emotional issues; how hard it was to stop the cycling brain from reliving it over and over again with a sense of justice – and in our case – without finding the murderer.

I told them about the hidden rage. At the time, a reporter, Tom Blackwell, had written about it. In the article, *Families of homicide victims admit dark thoughts of revenge,* one member, Ronald, had been quoted. "Sometimes I used to dream about how I would torture him. But he would die on me, and I would get mad and go and ask the doctor to bring him back to life – so I could do it all over."

I told them about the compulsion to make sense of it, how I had found myself telling the story in front of the mirror if there was no one to talk to. I told them how devastating it was to find my social circle changing – some ostracizing – some understanding – and how precious was every sympathetic word. I described my hunger for understanding – and the enormous fear to prevent it from happening again. I wanted to build a fortress around our family. Most of all, I wanted to know who had done it.

Later on, I would enhance my seven points, and add:
uncovering the guilt
fixing the harm
restoring relationships
finding meaning
placing the memory
finding perspective
letting go, accepting
looking ahead

Meanwhile, as all of this was happening, I was still concerned about the broader question – why did we forgive? It bothered me that eighty percent of the country was misreading us – thinking that we were unconcerned about the vulnerable in our society.

What did forgiveness mean to me?

I'm a writer – I had to write it all down to process it.

After that there seemed to be a growing demand for my story. There were always three points – the fear of the shapeshifting cloud – the rage of wanting to kill ten child murderers – and my need to forgive.

I was embracing it and talking about it.

I was beginning to preach it.

In our attempt to create and deliver justice, we have concentrated only on determining guilt. We have given the courtroom entirely to the professionals who have made it into a sterile room of law and order. As in the past, they have banned the fainting father from the room and silenced the screaming mother. More and more, they are whisking the difficult decision-making process away from the public into the realm of plea bargaining, with the same intentions as the doctors in keeping the baby clean and safe, out of the weak mother's arms. Consequently, we now have offenders and victims experiencing the trauma of the courtroom. We need the same delivery room revolution to happen in the courtroom.

A year later, we organized a second Justice Program meeting, hoping to duplicate the meeting we had with the hundred inmates.

This time Marie was going to participate.

We chose three storytellers – just as we had before. Since we had set out a good model for a meeting, I thought it would just happen, so I had given the organization of it to our director at the time.

This time there was no table – no barriers. Only seven inmates were chosen to participate.

Then the head of the inmates had insisted on forming a large circle.

Circles are great for ensuring a balance of power but not for an intervention between victims and offenders. Worse yet, the circle sharing was dominated by the inmates telling their stories – intimidating the survivors. They told their stories first.

I was caught as a powerless spectator. I was mortified as I saw it unfold.

It was the re-victimization that we had all been afraid of.

Their black clouds had won over ours – and it had been a slaughter.

We would never do that again.

Chapter 9
FIRST BREAKFAST

I looked up.

Somehow – and I wasn't sure how – my article was done and sent off.

I looked outside. I had stayed late – my husband had looked after the children, and I had lost precious time with them.

The sky was now one giant, dark cloud of misery, still rolling around, taunting me.

I was troubled in a new, worrisome way. I had lost an entire afternoon because of my black trauma…. The clouds were taking control again.

Why, I wondered. I had met all kinds of offenders. Then I realized the difference. They had been on the inside behind the walls – controlled. René was on the outside.

He had access to young people. With the platform of Restorative Justice, he was given power. The movement was creating cracks in the wall. It was breaking down the code of silence between victim and offender. They weren't adhering to the rule of "no uncontrolled contacts" that the justice system had so carefully built between the warring factions.

I had no idea that they would couple me with a notorious offender. When I had been approached by the organizers of the school to speak to the students, I had wondered if it was a good idea. Considering my busy schedule, looming deadlines, I had my doubts.

But then I had rationalized. The school was close by. I could do it during my lunch break – one hour in and out. Students were impressionable. I remembered all the school speakers I had enjoyed during my high school years. It was an opportunity to do good – again.

The organizers had mentioned that they were dedicating a whole day to the concept of restorative justice, but they hadn't said anything more. I suspected that's why they wanted me to balance it out with crime victim awareness. And I appreciated their sensitivity.

When I had arrived, there had been a sense of anticipation.

They led me to the class, whispering excitedly behind me. The classroom I had been assigned to was brimming to capacity with students and teachers alike.

I'm never quite sure of my audience until I see them. Seeing all these students, roughly the same age as Candace, filled me with passion. I told them all about Candace and about her love for her friends. I could see them melt. I warned them to make the most of every day and to love their parents who loved them. I taught them that forgiveness was a mysterious alternative of turning every ugly experience into a good memory.

After my presentation, the organizers insisted I stay to hear the next speaker who was going to speak in the gymnasium.

They even introduced me to Durocher just before he stepped onto the stage. I told him that I might have to leave early – given my deadlines.

He nodded.

I took a chair in the back of the auditorium, and I was glad I did.

I was spellbound by his story and horrified at the same time. I was fully aware that, to keep the students' attention, he needed to be dramatic, to sensationalize his story. But had he fallen into the temptation of glorifying crime? I felt the dark forces hovering around me – starting to swirl….

Had it really come to this? Was I now sharing the conference platform with a wild French-Canadian man? Were we now nothing but a dog and pony show?

I slipped out the back door.

Hurricane forgiveness!

When I was being introduced to him, we had shaken hands. I'm still not sure if I extended mine first – or had he? In any case, if he knew that I was a crime victim, he would also have known our secret code. We do not shake hands. And even worse than that was the fact that he was favored. I had spoken in a small classroom – he had the entire gymnasium.

Not that I wanted a gymnasium – I didn't like to speak to an audience of any size. Yet the moment was not lost on me. His offender story had overpowered my victim story.

The real question was: Does someone change from once being the "Most Wanted Criminal in Canada" – a dangerous, gun-carrying, bank robber – into a good, good father?

Meeting the inmates in prison didn't pose the same threat – they were locked in. This man was free to move around society.

If he hadn't changed and if I didn't say anything – I would be enabling a violent man to continue his violence.

And to tell the truth, I didn't believe him.

As victims, we become truth serums. We have a well-developed sixth sense of who is guilty and who isn't. Who is good and who isn't.

Even if the organizers had been conned, I hadn't.

Despite his thick – very thick – French-Canadian accent, he connected with the young crowd. These were hormonal young people – a difficult crowd to talk to at the best of times. Yet he had held them in the palm of his hand. He had them in his complete control....

That's what was bothering me! Was he just a good storyteller, or was he a manipulator as he exploited the drama of his story? Was he creating genuine change in society? Or was it just a ploy? What were his real intentions? Did we know?

This was dangerous.

I had never heard of anyone changing their minds, values and attitudes just because of a wife and children. It needed to be a

Damascus experience. Light – conversion – those were the stories I was used to – this had none of it. This was an exceptional crime, committed by a man with exceptional charisma – and a ho-hum change attached.

Everyone had warned me that the uncharted restorative justice movement was unsafe for victims. Was this the proof of that?

I had no choice.

I had the feeling that this was not going to be a one-time event. Restorative Justice was interested in our stories.

If we were going to be a dog and pony show – I would need to know.

I found Durocher's contact information.

I picked up the telephone.

Would he meet me for breakfast?

I would pay.

The clouds followed me home that night…. They were always with me. They haunted me for the entire week as I waited for our breakfast.

I was one hot mess of nerves when I walked into the restaurant that morning to meet him.

Suddenly the compulsion to meet him was wavering. Did I really want to do this? Meet with him alone?

He was already sitting in the back of the restaurant when I arrived – in exactly the place I would have chosen.

We were probably the two most unlikely people ever to meet and have a breakfast conversation.

He was French, a Catholic born in Montreal, Quebec. I was British, a Mennonite born in Chilliwack, British Columbia.

He was a bank robber, a well-known criminal, violent, and ruthless. I was a parent of a murdered child, law-abiding, pacifist, and conscientious.

I had been sheltered – he was street smart.

He had grown up breaking the law to survive. I was pious to the extreme. I hadn't even smoked a cigarette behind a barn – much less stolen anything.

He had robbed a bank – driven by greed. I was from a modest, frugal family that felt money was the "root of all evil."

I slid into the booth opposite him.

He looked smaller than on the stage – darker somehow – less impressive.

We just looked at each other for the first moment.

How does one open this kind of conversation? It didn't seem appropriate to talk about the weather.

Actually, there was little time for idle chitchat anyway. I had scheduled this breakfast very early in the morning at 6:00 a.m. because my days were already full – too full.

I had a full-time job, two children, a demanding volunteer commitment, speaking engagements, and I was still working through piles of leftover grief and trauma.

I really didn't have time for this…nor did I want to make the time. I was tired – almost to the point of exhaustion.

This was going to be a simple in and out – no time for chitchat.

"Thank you for meeting me," I said as a starter.

My black cloud had turned into a warrior – tense.

He nodded. He must have sensed it.

The waitress hovered. We both ordered – something simple – coffee and two pieces of toast. He ordered rye bread.

I shoved the cutlery aside and laid down my notebook. "I asked you out for breakfast," I began formally, "because I have a few questions."

He nodded. "I will answer any question you want to ask. I will try to answer them as honestly as I can," he said, unsmiling. He looked defensive – wary.

I suddenly realized how he must feel – having to meet me – a well-known crime victim. I probably represented "the law" to him – the unforgiving public.

I softened. "You are a great storyteller," I said. "The students hung onto your every word."

He nodded but still didn't smile.

Perhaps he sensed that he was about to go under an inquisition of sorts. Perhaps it was prudent for him to be on his guard – I was prepared to hold every one of his words against him.

I cleared my throat.

I had two questions.

I started with the first.

"When did you start robbing banks?" I asked, taking a sip of my coffee that had been delivered by a seemingly nervous waitress. Everyone seemed nervous.

He looked hesitant – as if my question was unexpected – too forward.

I offered another question. "Were you in your twenties when you started robbing banks?"

"I didn't start with robbing banks. I started shoplifting as a child."

I expected as much – but I wasn't interested in him as a child.

"But when did you get serious about robbing banks?" I pushed.

"I got my first handgun when I was thirteen years old. I paid fifty, maybe a hundred dollars for the gun – money from small shoplifting that I had been doing. Then I started pulling armed robberies in the corner stores."

"A gun at thirteen?"

"Yes."

I didn't say anything – just looked at him – trying to imagine life at thirteen with a gun.

I was remembering when I was thirteen years old. I had attended high school, getting on a bus for a thirty-minute drive from Greendale to Clearbrook to attend a private school, Mennonite Educational Institute. We wore navy uniforms with white blouses.

Candace, our daughter, was thirteen years old when she was murdered. She had been like me. She, too attended a private school, Mennonite Brethren Collegiate Institute here in Winnipeg – just down the street from our home.

We were leading boring, innocent lives, while he had been out shopping for a gun at thirteen?

Our worlds were colliding on many levels.

I took a deep breath, shoved my memories aside, and listened as he continued.

"After I bought the gun, me and the guys would go out into the woods to practice. To shoot, you had to know your gun, be able to load it quickly. We would practice shooting at birds and trees. I learned to know my gun very well."

I just stared at him. I didn't really even know what kind of answers I wanted from him. I just wanted him to talk so I could watch him – study him. I had slipped into my journalist mode – pretending he was just another source interview, and I was researching crime.

"After getting your gun, you started robbing…?" I let the question trail away. Sometimes open-ended reflective questions, hints, or suggestions would just get them talking…. They could finish the sentence with anything they wanted.

It worked.

He seemed to sink further into his memories, just as I had hoped.

"I was known as the tough kid in the neighborhood. It is what I did."

Then he began to describe his life on the streets – all the stores he had robbed. His mother was poor. It is what he needed to do.

"What did it feel like," I asked, "to own a gun?"

"When I got the gun?"

His face lit up. "Oh my god! Every time I pointed the gun at someone, I felt the power. It was like being a race car driver with the best car in the world."

"So, it felt good?"

He smiled for the first time. "And then there was my switchblade knife. I'd stick it into my waistband – easy to grab with my right hand. Even if it was invisible, everyone knew it was there. And nobody wanted to approach you! No one in the neighborhood could say that I was a chicken. I was not afraid of anyone or anything."

He seemed transported back in time.

"My life was full of hate. My gun became the extension of my violence, my hatred. I didn't only feel it, I made a point of exuding hatred. I really worked at my image. Everything I did, the way I talked, the way I walked, even the way I dressed, all said, 'Don't approach me.'

"When I started doing robberies, I met a guy who was almost as daring and crazy as I was. He was older, yet I took the lead. I was the brave, macho kid, so I just told him, 'Hey, follow me,' and he did. We were the perfect team."

This was his survival, and apparently, he had learned it well. He described it over again and over again. I leaned forward and listened intently, trying to visualize him as a child – a rebel child – always testing the boundaries.

Then the mood changed. It was as if he was now seeing me – testing me with his story. His eyes grew dark. "I was happy when people hated me. If they hated me, it meant that they were afraid of me. Violence attracted me."

I could feel his dangerous side. His eyes grew even darker.

I knew that I was encountering the man behind the mask.

This was why I had asked him here. I wanted to know if he was really a criminal – if he had the ability to intimidate – to execute the crime he had claimed to do.

Now I knew – and I could feel the first shiver of fear.

He continued. "I was only fourteen when my sister, who was singing at a nightclub, needed a bouncer, so I volunteered to be her bouncer. I just sat there, listening to her. She sounded like Doris Day. I didn't drink. I didn't like booze even back then.

"I would put my gun on the table and watch. If there was trouble, I would say, 'You have two choices. You are leaving…or else.' If I told the guy to lie down on the floor, he would. All I would say is, 'If you don't, I will shoot you.' I felt so powerful, watching over my older sister and taking care of her. In the end, I didn't shoot anyone. It was all just threats – but it worked. Everyone called me 'Mister.'"

I could see him. "Then what?"

"At fourteen years of age, I started wearing stocking masks to do the robberies. No one could recognize me because the stocking flattens your nose, your face. People were afraid of me. I wasn't a nervous kid. I would say, 'Get down. Open the till.' People would freeze from fear.

"After the till is open, taking the money is the easy part. I would just take the big bills – $5, $10, $20. There weren't many $100 bills in the corner stores.

"The quicker you get in, the quicker you get out. I did most of the robberies by myself at that point."

I don't think I said much after that. I was just taking mental notes as he told me his story and then retold me the same story in different ways. I didn't even know which questions to ask, his world was so different than mine.

Was he telling me the truth – or was this all a lie?

I glanced at my watch. It was late. I picked up my notebook. The pages were blank.

I was exhausted. I couldn't think of anything more.

I thanked him profusely for answering my questions.

I got up – he followed me.

I paid the bill at the front.

It was all extremely awkward.

Whatever answer I had been looking for – I hadn't found it.

I wasn't convinced he had changed.

He still bothered me….

It wasn't that he had done anything to me – he hadn't offended me. It was what he represented – the entitled criminals.

Not only entitled – but dangerous.

I was exhausted – even that hostile presence that had reared its ugly head the entire visit – seemed to be tired.

Chapter 10
SECOND BREAKFAST

I looked up from my desk, surprised that the wind had picked up and was whipping the snow into a frenzy.

Winter was coming with a vengeance again. It reminded me of that crazy blizzard of white, swirling snow that had greatly reduced visibility the day Candace disappeared – possibly the reason a predator could force her off the road. It was the same kind of snow squall that had followed the funeral procession to the cemetery.

These blizzards always brought back memories.

A few weeks later, I still couldn't lay the breakfast to rest.

The night before, when I had attended the survivors support meeting, I had described my meeting with René, his story, and some of my doubts.

They were horrified that I would even have breakfast with him.

"You believe him?" they asked incredulously.

"I don't know. What do you think?"

"People don't change!" they insisted. "And now that he is out of prison, he's even more dangerous."

They also let me know, in no uncertain terms, what they thought of Restorative Justice – it wasn't safe either.

There was no safe place they insisted. They had the same perception of the Criminal Justice System. They just had no place to go to.

Now I had 130 people who were depending on me....

Was I being conned? Was Restorative Justice being conned?
Had he changed? Was he dangerous?
If he hadn't changed – I would need to warn others.
I had no choice.
I had to stop it.
I found Durocher's contact information.
I picked up the telephone.
Would he meet me for breakfast?
"Yes," he said, just as he had before – no questions asked.
I set the time.
I wondered if I had lost my mind.
I would pay.

I didn't feel any better about this second breakfast meeting than I had about the first. I was still one hot mess of nerves, hoping no one would notice me walking into the restaurant to have another breakfast with him.

The first time was bad enough, this second time could be seen as establishing a pattern.

He was already sitting in the same place as last time.

One thing was easy – we seemed to have no problem setting up a meeting. He liked an early morning breakfast – I could suggest any time after 6:00 a.m. he said. My office was close to restaurants on his way to his work.

I slid into the booth opposite him.

For a moment, he just watched me. I watched him. There was no smile. This was all business. Our separate clouds were watching each other.

"Thank you for meeting me again," I said.

He nodded.

The waitress hovered. We both ordered – something simple again – same thing – coffee and two pieces of toast. He ordered rye bread.

We were both creatures of habit.

I shoved the cutlery aside and laid down my notebook. "I asked you out for breakfast," I began formally, "because I have a few more questions."

He nodded. "I will answer any question you want to ask. I will try to answer them as honestly as I can," he said sincerely, but unsmiling, just as he had been before.

In my scant research on offenders, I had learned that many of them had experienced abuse – especially at the hands of their father, so I thought I might start there.

"Tell me about your childhood," I said.

"My childhood?" he asked incredulously.

"Yes – as if you were writing an autobiography…time and place of birth. Insights into your parents. Things like that."

This time my pen was poised.

Without hesitation, he plunged into his story.

"My story really starts with my parents. My mother's name was Jeannette, my father's name was René."

"Namesake?"

"Actually, I was named after my brother, who died as a baby just before I came along. Why she did that – I'll never know. It didn't make things easy for me – to feel like a replacement baby. She also named me after my father whom she hated."

"Hated her husband?" I asked.

"Yes – she hated him. He left her for another woman. I wondered why anyone would name their seventh child after the man they hated. And then if I did anything, she was unhappy with, she would say, 'You are just like your father!' She reminded me of how she felt about her husband – and me – constantly."

"What was your father like? Why did she hate him?" I asked. I was probably being a bit obvious the way I was looking for a troubled relationship. I assumed all offenders would have trouble with their fathers. Even average-functioning, healthy males seemed to have trouble with their fathers. I remembered when my husband, who was studying masculinity at the time, would ask all the men we met if they had a good relationship with their father. Many of them burst into tears....

He was hesitating.

"Did you have a good relationship with your father?" I asked again.

"Until I was five years old, I didn't even know who my father was or what that word even meant. You don't know a father who hasn't been around, who has never taken you into his arms or put you to bed."

There was a wistfulness.... He didn't burst into tears – but there was pain in his eyes. Then he continued.

"He had actually left my mother way before I was born. I think he was coming home to see the children, or whatever, and then they would end up in bed, and she would have another baby. This was his history. He would come home, use our mother and...and never really stayed to be a father to the children. It was a love-hate relationship. It was what my mother had for him. Conflicted."

"So, you never saw him at all?" I was wondering if his abuse, victimization, would be classified as neglect – something that I understood could be as harmful to a child's self-esteem as outright violent abuse.

He shook his head. "My few memories I have of him was of their constant fighting. I couldn't understand the tension at the time. Now I understand. My father had made a life with another woman, and I don't know how many children he had with her, so when he did come, there was tension. I'm left with the early memories of the endless fighting in the house. My mother always said she hated him...."

I watched him.

"Was there abuse?" I probed.

"My most vivid memory – that still sticks with me – is the time the argument turned into violence. I can still see – vividly – my father picking up a knife and lunging at my mom to stab her. She ducked, and the blade hit the wall. When his hand hit the wall, the knife slipped and he sliced his hand – cutting all the tendons in his fingers. He was yelling, she was screaming, and all I remember is that from that day on, I can only see the blood, hear the screaming. It never left me."

We paused. I started writing it down. He sipped his coffee.

Frankly, it was hard for me to imagine the scene or understand domestic fighting. My parents had never fought. They had this wonderful habit of sitting in the shade of the barn on a warm evening and chatting to each other. But there was only one incident imprinted on my mind when I had noticed something. I must have been around six years of age. My mother had been unusually restless, pacing from the kitchen into the dining room, always pausing to look outside the window to the Shell service station across the yard where my father worked. Finally, taking off her apron, she walked across the yard to the garage – hesitated, drew in a big breath and walked in. She didn't even notice me following, curious.

My father had been surprised to see her and put down his tools. They went into the parts section of the garage, and then they had talked. I think there were tears.

That was my one and only experience of parental discord – very different from his. If I could still remember…no wonder he could remember his.

He continued. "I was about six years old. My two younger brothers were sleeping. Bernard was about one year old, and Jean was about three. I was the only one not taking an afternoon nap, so I was the only one to see this. I remember screaming and crying, and watching all that blood spurting out all over…. I remember wanting to protect my mother. I remember hating my father. I took on the responsibility of that moment – but I was powerless. I couldn't protect her. I could only scream. I think that marked my life."

His eyes were very dark.

"I hated my father from that day on. I hated him with a passion."

"Do you still see it – the scene?"

"The slash, the blood, the scream…that is what sticks with me to this day.

"As a child, one of the first things, my most vivid memory is of that knife going into the wall, and you don't know how to take it. I imagine my mother took me in her arms to try to comfort me but…. I don't know what my father did. He probably left right away. I know that the screaming stopped. There was blood on the floor and the wall, but there was no more screaming between the two of them. That one scene affected me. I hated my father ever after – and I wanted revenge."

"When did you see him again?"

"A year and a half later, when I was at the convent, he came to visit us – my sister and me. He had changed. I was surprised at the sight of him. He had a mustache. He wasn't the huge man I remember. He was only a little bit taller than I was. It was like he was a stranger and I was meeting a stranger. The only way that I was certain it was my father was when I saw his hand. It was deformed. He was not able to close his hand. When you are a kid, you forget the face of the person and stuff like this, so it was a shock to see him – and see that his hand had closed permanently."

"What did you say to him?"

"I spoke to him for two seconds, just long enough to tell him that I never wanted to see him again."

"And did you see him again?"

"No," he shook his head. "But even just the sound of his name brought out the rage in me. The next time I heard about him was when I was at my mother's place, and one of my sisters came home and told my mother that she had seen my father walking down the street. I just ran out of the house, slamming the door behind and went to look for him. I just wanted to beat the shit out of him. Even just the mention of his name would send me into a fit of rage."

"Did you find him?"

"I never found him. Glad I didn't. I always told myself that I would never be like him. I always saw the bad part of my father –

never the good part. I am sure he had a good part…but I never saw it. I just was filled with hate – and this deep void for a father figure. All I could think of was beating the shit out of my father – for letting me down – moving out of my life – never giving me any father model to live by – no support. I truly disowned him."

"What about your mother?" I asked.

"My mother failed me too…or at least that is the conclusion I came to. She couldn't provide for us as children. After my father's bloody assault, my mother went to work at a place where they were killing chickens, as well as an assistant nurse at the hospital. She worked two jobs."

Then he smiled. "To survive it all, she became a kind of dictator. We had to do what she wanted, or we would get it. No doubt. She wanted to control everything! She was a control freak. I guess she didn't know any better."

He paused. "Then it went from bad to worse. Shortly after that event, my mother was diagnosed with cancer. They gave her six months to live. She had a bag on her side for the rest of her life. She was bitter, she was angry. She had no choice but to place us in care."

I glanced at my watch. I needed to get back to the office. I didn't have the time to ask him about a lengthy process – nor did I want to know.

I just wanted to know "if" he had truly changed.

I searched for the right question – that definitive question that would reveal his heart to me.

Then I knew. "Would you ever rob another bank?" I asked.

It felt like a tired question – I was tired of this all.

He paused – weighing his words carefully. "I can't say I would never rob another bank. There are no guarantees in life. I don't know what I'll do ten years from now – even next week." He paused again – his gaze steady.

"But I can tell you that I don't want to rob another bank in my life. I can also tell you that I won't rob a bank today. I can only answer for the day. Today is all I have."

81

I stared at him. He had just admitted that he wasn't the normal, victimized convict. He was driven by money. He was addicted to the good life. He had an inclination to steal – to break the law – that was like an addiction.

There were no excuses, no promises, no denial, none of that. His words matched the reality of who he was.

Even though there was a canyon between us, I felt that I could finally trust him. He had integrity – at least at that moment, he had integrity. It was all that he would promise.

I had a new…understanding.

Our aggressive clouds almost shook hands.

"Thank you," I said simply and picked up my notebook, which had notes in it this time. "I need to get back to the office, but I thank you for what you've just told me."

Again, I paid the bill at the front. I thanked him profusely – then said good-bye to him.

Perhaps change was possible?

Time would tell.

Chapter 11
PSYCHOPATH

Time did tell.

Time always has a way of sorting things out.

It was three years later.

I attended Congress 1995 of the Criminal Justice Association of Canada held in Winnipeg at the grand, historic Fort Garry Hotel.

I came a bit early to set up and wandered upstairs looking for my workshop room.

I remember meandering up to the mezzanine which served as the perfect focal point to watch the comings and goings of the attendees. On the main floor, I spotted René Durocher – in a suit – mingling with the guests – working the room.

The hotel had a soaring, two-story lobby with a stone staircase, brass railings, and beautiful chandeliers. He looked as if he belonged – talking and laughing with everyone, guests and organizers, greeting them all as if they were long-lost friends. He seemed on top of his game.

A young man coming up the stairs waved to me and then joined me at the railing. I recognized him from some of the restorative justice symposiums that I had attended. "And, how are you?" he asked.

"Not so good – I'm supposed to present a workshop entitled 'Church and Crime Victims' to this crowd and I have no idea what I am expected to say or why I was chosen for this topic…," I said in frustration.

He smiled. "I know. I was the one that chose you and the topic."

"Why?" I said in horror. "No one here will be interested in my views on the church. This is Corrections – who deal with inmates. Prisons. The church isn't important to their population, and church isn't important to crime victims either."

"But church is important to you…. Tell us why." He was edging away with an odd twinkle in his eye – always irresistible as he charmed his way around the most difficult situations. He would go far in this his chosen field.

"I'll be asking more questions than I answer," I called after him.

"Be yourself," he smiled as he went to join the others.

René spotted me and came running up the stairs.

"Willie Gibbs wants to speak to you. I don't know where he is right now, but I will introduce you to him when I find him." He paused to grab a breath. "He wants to talk to you!"

He repeated it again. "He really wants to talk to you!" As if that was the most special thing in the world.

"And who is Willie Gibbs?" I asked.

"He was the Warden of Springhill Institution in Nova Scotia when I was there. He was the Senior Deputy Commissioner of the Correctional Service of Canada and became the Chairman of the National Parole Board."

Apparently, I was supposed to be impressed.

And then René was swept away – mingling with the others.

I just watched.

I didn't know anyone in this crowd – and I wasn't even sure that I wanted to. This was definitely not my crowd of people. They were all in Corrections – enemy territory.

But they seemed to want something from me. What did they want? What did I want?

I attended some workshops – listened to some of the presentations – but mainly waited until it was time to deliver my own workshop.

I was surprised that the room was full. I began by confessing my frustration with the topic, and then just shared my journey openly –

and they just smiled. They didn't seem to mind that I didn't have any answers…. They just wanted to discuss the issues.

Does faith have a role in the rehabilitation of offenders – in the healing of the victims – and if so, how do we introduce it? I thought it did. As confused as I was – I still knew it was my faith in forgiveness that would see me through. I could talk about that.

It didn't seem to matter what I said. They were polite – and smiling. It was quite wonderful.

Later that day, just before I was about to leave, I was approached by a rather gentle, tall man. "I'm Willie Gibbs," he said, extending his hand.

"I've been told about you," I smiled. "I think we have someone in common – René Durocher."

He nodded and burst into the biggest smile – as if I had just mentioned the name of his star student.

He said that he had been warden of one of the prisons when René was an inmate.

I remember thinking that he was far too gentle to be the warden of a prison. All the wardens that I was meeting were wise and almost tender. I couldn't imagine them dealing with a prison revolt or even a lockdown.

He wanted to know about my work with crime victims – and my organized encounters. I remember telling him the positive aspects – but owning my own confusion and questions.

He said something about my positive influence on René.

I didn't know what he was talking about. I didn't really have that much to do with René, and I said as much. He just smiled.

I saw his comments as an opening to ask my biggest question.

"If you knew him well in prison," I asked, "can you tell me what he was like?"

Gibbs grinned. "He was nasty…just nasty. He was probably the most dangerous inmate we had. He wasn't the usual convict. Because he wasn't a user and never did any drugs, he didn't need anything.

There was nothing that we had to control him. He lived on anger – and hated everyone. He could fight – lie – and out-manipulate us all."

Gibbs shook his head as he remembered. "He truly operated only on hate."

"Do you think someone like that can change?" I asked.

"Yes, I do. I've seen it. I don't know how, but he did it. I do believe he has changed."

"Really?"

He nodded. "Yes, he's changed. I think we would know by now if he hadn't. There are a few of us here at the Congress who have experienced him as changed."

Then we went through it all again – he repeated it over and over. René had been the worst.

Subtly, I asked a few more questions about René – mainly to check out his stories – and they checked out. I had a first-hand witness.

Then, seeing his taxi at the door, Gibbs took the time to encourage me in my work. Shook my hand again.

I watched him – fascinated. Curious. What was this all about? And what was my role?

I noticed that René was still chatting with the guests…. He had been watching my meeting with Gibbs.

He came over immediately. He would have liked to debrief, but it was getting late – I was tired.

"Coffee?" I asked.

"Breakfast?" he asked with a hint of a smile.

We made arrangements to meet at the same place near Polo Park in a few days. I had so many more questions now….

This time I had an agenda – I had seen a new René – he was connected.

I thought there might be one solution for my cloud situation. Perhaps if we knew who the murderer of Candace was – this cloud would dissipate.

I was remembering another expert. I remembered how an ex-con had come to our door – late at night – during the time of Candace's disappearance.

He explained his mission quickly.

"You don't know anything," he began bluntly. "You lead a sheltered life. How do you know what criminals think? What do you know about street life?"

We had to agree with him.

"Maybe I have something you need. I know how criminals think." Never in my life had I thought that his nine years behind bars might be an asset, a kind of specialization.

"What do you think?" we asked.

"I think you will find her body close to home."

I stalled. "Personally, I think she was probably picked up with a car. She could be out of the city by now."

"That's where you are wrong," he countered. "These types of criminals don't do things like that. They stay where they are. They don't travel around much."

He stood up. "Come on, I'll show you."

Then the man had taken Cliff and my father around the entire community, identifying drug pushers' houses, the homes of Bravo Motorcycle Club members. He also pointed out many shelters, camper trailers, sheds, and heated garages that should be searched.

And he had been right! Candace had been found close by in an abandoned shed.

René was an ex-con – he might know something. He would know how criminals think.

René slid into the booth opposite me. The café was filling up with people – ordinary people having breakfast, having what I assumed were ordinary conversations.

This was anything but an ordinary conversation with René.

René wanted to know what I thought of Willie Gibbs – his eyes were shining. Obviously, Gibbs was his favorite, all-time hero.

As we ordered, we talked about the Congress – and René described everything he had done to help organize.

I listened…but that's not what I wanted to know…. I wanted to know his inner thoughts.

I appealed to his love for the story. "What was it like to go into prison for the first time? What was your strategy?"

René paused…. It took only seconds, and he plunged into his storytelling mode.

"I didn't panic. I knew that I would only be in prison for a while – only two years, and then I would be out. So, I cut myself off from everything. I did not even have a visitors list. I didn't want to see anybody. There were no visits. But having visitors was a privilege. If you didn't do your chores or if you acted out, your visits were cut off. I said, 'Go ahead. Cut off my visits. I don't have visitors anyway. Stick it.' I didn't want anything. I know my brother tried to visit me, but I turned him down. There was nothing that I wanted to have from anybody. I was an animal.

"Nobody had a hold on me. You can't force someone to do anything if they just don't care. When you don't care if you live or die, when you have nothing in life to live for, you can't be manipulated. I got to a point – that I didn't care if I would be killed by someone stronger than me or someone with more guts than me, or crazier than me. It is the way I was. I felt it was the honorable way to live – or die – given the situation I was in.

"Then six months later, I heard that my partner, the guy I trusted with my life, who had left me lying in the street, had been charged with something else and was now in the same penitentiary.

"I was pissed with him…. I value loyalty. From the very beginning, when I had started doing small robberies, I expected people to do exactly what I told them to do. My word was law, and if you breached that word, I would get the person back one day. He left me lying there in the street. I would have put my life on the line for him and I expected him to do the same for me. If something had happened to my partner in the bank, if someone had jumped him, I was prepared to shoot. I would do it instinctively. I had trained my mind.

"When I heard that my partner was inside the prison. Oh my god! I arranged with the guards for him to come into the yard, and I gave it to him. I just beat the shit out of him. It was not enough to just punch and kick him. 'I am so thrilled to see you, you son of a bitch. You should have never done that. You left me there as if I was dead. When I asked you to take me with you, you never did.'

"I was so full of anger and hate that I couldn't stop myself. I just gave it to him and gave it to him and beat him to a pulp. He ended up in the hospital.

"He never went out in the population after that. Never.

"But the guards – grabbed me and put me in the hole.

"The hole in those days was different than it is now. That's where they put you when you breach the rules. You can get fifteen days, thirty or forty-five days in the hole. When you are sentenced to thirty days in the hole, you are served eight slices of bread a day, and every seven days you get a meal. Imagine – one meal every seven days! The rest of the time they give you only bread. The only thing you can keep in your cell is a towel. After taking your shower, you wrap your bread up in it and make a pillow out of it. You don't want to eat dry bread or even fresh bread without anything else. I just said, 'Stick it. I don't care.' I was so disciplined and self-controlled. I never ate the bread. It was more useful as a pillow. They gave me a book – a Bible. I never opened a page. Never. I didn't want anything from anybody. I was so angry and filled with hatred. I hated the people of God.

"I know. I was declared a psychopath in the penitentiary. Maybe I was. Maybe I was not. I don't know because I didn't even know the meaning of the word psychopath. I graduated from Grade Seven. Although I attended Grade Nine for a while, I quit school after that and never went back. My education was quite limited. Even when

I was in school, I didn't study at all. So, I didn't know what that meant."

I just watched him. He seemed even less guarded than the last time.

He continued to reminisce. "They gave me medication. Because they think you are crazy, they never open your cell door, unless you are going to see a doctor. They wanted to calm me with 'bug juice' – medication dissolved in water – but I threw it against the wall. I always said, 'What the fuck do you want, you fuckin'…. Fuck you. I am not crazy. You are crazy.' I was just angry. 'You are fuckin' crazy. Leave me the fuck alone. Leave me in my cell. I don't care if I ever get out.' I didn't care. You get to the point where you become comfortable in your cell. You never have to do anything."

I had seen a glimpse of the old René – the René in jail. It wasn't hard to believe the warden now.

He continued. "I tried to prove to them that I was a real psychopath. Everything I did was to show I was more violent than anyone else. No one was violent towards me. It was the kind of jungle I had lived in since I was five years old. I protected myself by being violent towards others. I made my point. They knew that if they came at me, I would fuckin' kill them."

There it was. This is what Willie Gibbs had been talking about. The stories were lining up.

René pushed his coffee back.

He studied me for a long time. "You know – I think you have questions that I can't answer. You are looking for something. What are you looking for?"

He was right. There was a question I had never asked him. In fact, I had never talked much about my case with him. It was mainly me asking about him.

This was one of his first questions about me.

I studied him. Did I dare? I formed the question in my mind. "Do you know the details of our case – the murder of our daughter?" I asked.

90

He shrugged. "Wasn't in Winnipeg at the time, but I know some of it."

"My daughter was murdered, and they still haven't found anyone.... It's been ten years."

He nodded.

I leaned forward. "You are in prison. You know everyone – the officials, the guards, and the prisoners. You are part of that culture. I know that people talk. I'm sure they've talked about our case in prison. My question is: What are they saying?"

He looked a little cornered – as if he was sorting what would be appropriate to tell me and what wouldn't. I knew some of the talk.... I could only imagine what he had heard.

"They talk," he shrugged – obviously discarding some of it as irrelevant talk. "But I don't know that much about your case. In prison, there are different places for different crimes. The man who killed your daughter – he would have been a sick puppy. That's what I call them," he shrugged dismissively. "I don't know anything about that section. They are separated from the regular population."

But then he looked at me with a new tenderness. I think that is the word for it. He was looking at me as if I was a child. As if he understood how desperate I was to know.... "They are sick puppies?" I reflected the question back to him.

"Yes – they are sick puppies. They can't be cured. They are sick."

"But what do you think about our case? Anything...."

It was as if he could see through me to the underlying question – which I didn't even know was there.

I could feel the black cloud's breath. I could smell it.

"You couldn't have stopped it from happening, Wilma. If you had picked her up that day, he would have chosen another day. They choose. They stalk. They are sick puppies."

I wasn't sure if he was right or not – I didn't know. I'm not sure it was much comfort to know if Candace had been stalked or not.

But I did have a sense that he knew. It did take care of some guilt. At least he didn't blame me – not like some others had....

I had one more question. "I believe he has killed himself. I believe that he couldn't have lived with himself after that…. Do you think he is alive?"

René shook his head. "It is good to tell yourself that – but people like that don't kill themselves. They are too afraid to die. He will keep his secret."

I sighed. It was one thing to deal with my own inner trauma and demons; it was another thing to deal with the haunting presence of the murderer.

Would I ever be free?

Chapter 12
LIFERS' LOUNGE

It was a few months after that I found myself in the CJOB waiting room. We were to go on air in a few minutes but René was nowhere to be seen.

Our radio host emerged from the studio. Greeted me but noticed – "Isn't René here?"

I shook my head.

This was awkward. René was always early.

René was a favorite at CJOB. The Open Line radio show had started with host Peter Warren, who had a particular interest in crime, who had been with the show for twenty-five years. For Warren, it wasn't only about reporting on crime, he became involved. In fact, four escaped convicts had given themselves up to him on air…and he had a lengthy correspondence with convicted child serial killer, Clifford Olson.

Peter Warren had heard that one of the students had asked René for his autograph and that René had refused saying, "You ask people like Wayne Gretzky for their autographs, not a guy like me." That convinced Warren that René was an example of a changed criminal and wanted to champion his cause.

Now, a new talk show host had asked us to be on his afternoon show. I think it was going to be an attempt to give the audience the experience of a genuine face-to-face victim and offender meeting – even if it was surrogate.

It was almost time to air when René appeared at the very last possible moment, running through the door – white as a sheet.

"I rolled my Malibu – grabbed a taxi – and I am here."

I stared at him – "You rolled your car?"

"It landed on the roof, and I got out through the front window. The ambulance was there in five minutes. They wanted to take me to the hospital. But I said, 'I have an appointment. I need a cab.' The ambulance phoned for a cab and here I am."

The host appeared. "We need to get on air."

"I'm okay," René said, drawing a deep breath as we followed him into the studio. Rene's hands were steady as he took his chair and put on the headphones.

As the host introduced us, I could see René steel himself – center himself – and become his usual animated storyteller.

I don't remember much of what we said. But I do know that there was one illustration that seemed to help people understand the need to have these victim-offender dialogues.

"We are bonded," I would say. "The man who murdered my daughter is like a member of our family. When I meet friends, they always politely ask after my husband Cliff – and I tell them that we are still married. And he is doing well.

"Then they ask about our daughter Odia – and she is also doing well. She is falling in love with Larry Reimer from Winkler, and then they ask about Syras, our youngest son – and I tell them that he is a potter like my husband….

"And then they pause – and ask about whether the case of the murder of our daughter has been solved.

"They are inquiring after Candace – but it is a question about the person who killed her. He is part of our story narrative. Even though we haven't a clue who he is, we have to accept him as part of our lives.

"In any case, we need to learn about them – like any other member of our family…. Become experts on them.

"The only way I can satisfy my need to know and be answerable is to connect with people who have criminal expertise – like René."

And we smiled at each other.

The radio host then looked directly at me, and I could tell that he was no longer a radio host.

"Wilma, you have said publicly that you forgive. How do you forgive the murder of your daughter? I am puzzled how a woman could forgive who has lost something so precious."

I tried to answer him. "Forgiveness is dealing with the issues. It's not wanting to kill them. It is wanting to understand…." And I went on and on about forgiveness. It was really my way of not getting stuck.

I don't think I satisfied his question, but we had to go on. He then asked René about his work.

René described his role as an Inreach worker – and how important it was for inmates to forgive themselves – and to receive forgiveness.

After the radio interview, René and I went for coffee to debrief.

I still had questions for him.

I realized that he had just told me three stories of when he'd tried to escape prison. It was curious that in each one – just as the plan was to be executed – something intervened at the very last moment. Days, even months of scheming and planning – all for naught.

Why was that?

I was also struck by his desperation.

His escape attempts had taken a great deal of time – patience – imagination.

He had been desperate.

But then again, I was desperate as well.

There are many ways to imprison the body, soul, and spirit of a person.

Odd – we were both going into our issues to free ourselves. He found freedom in his new program of helping lifers. I found mine in creating victim awareness.

"I guess we are both desperate," I murmured. "I'm desperate for answers – you are desperate still…."

He seemed to see me with new eyes.

"You are desperate?"

I nodded. "I still know nothing, René. Nothing."

He sat in silence for a long time, then he said, "Perhaps I have something that might be able to help you.... I have a lifers' group."

"Lifers?" I didn't understand the connection.

"I think you need to meet them and ask them the questions – not just me. When you go into prison – you are always looking after everyone. This time you need to come in alone. No one else – just you."

"I don't know how that will help me."

"It will," he promised. "It is what you need. It is what they need."

After a long moment of pondering, I finally nodded.

It was enough for him. "I will have to talk to the warden," he said.

It was a Monday evening, April 22, 1996.

The café was emptying as I had arrived – perhaps employees of the penitentiary, staff, and guards were leaving on their way back up the hill. I was glad to be alone.

There was no doubt that I was nervous. I had given myself plenty of time – allowing an hour to get to Stony Mountain Institution when it was only thirty kilometers from home – an easy twenty-five-minute drive.

I had at least a half-hour to kill.

My coffee came....

From where I sat, I could see the penitentiary. Intimidating as always! A fortress-like building over one hundred years old that had been built with Tyndall stone – impenetrable, meant to keep society safe by imprisoning the violent. It wasn't only meant to be a practical holding tank – but a message to everyone that there are means of controlling unwanted behavior. It had been built on a hill – rare on the prairies – a limestone outcropping thirty meters above the surrounding prairie.

There was a promise of spring even though the temperatures hovered around the freezing mark. All day I had heard about the ice jams – the cresting of the river. Everyone was happy though, since the slow thaw had diminished the threat of flooding – although the river had flooded a few houses.

My mind was cycling. How had I gotten myself into this – entrusting myself to the agenda of a bank robber – spending my time going into jail – exploring this part of society that I was so ill-equipped to deal with by myself?

I wondered what it would be like to meet with lifers.

Would my anger resurface?

Sitting there, looking up at the penitentiary, was triggering my memories. I remembered how a friend had come to visit a few months after Candace had been killed.

We hadn't seen each other for a while, and she told me about a few of the things she had gone through as a spectator of our experience.

She told me about her own questioning as to why this should happen to a friend, and I realized anew that our friends had gone through this with us. It was good to hear her anger, her perspective on the news coverage, and her theories about what might have happened.

She told me how she admired my forgiving spirit. "I know that you have forgiven. I sense no vengeance in you."

I wasn't as sure as she was that we had come to that resolution, but I was grateful for her words. I thanked her for her confidence. "We're trying," I said.

She asked if we were sleeping, if we were having nightmares.

"We're sleeping. We're having dreams, but not nightmares," I told her. I didn't tell her about the black cloud that seemed to come and go at will.

Her next question caught me off guard. "If you could let yourself go, what would satisfy justice for you? Would it be execution?"

I had never allowed myself the question. I didn't think I was ready to face the complexity of it. But I felt safe with her, and her question was an interesting one.

Perhaps it was time to think about it. I purposely loosened my controls and explored my inner feelings, my emotions. My friend waited in silence as I fell into deep thought.

"No," I finally answered, half to her and half to myself. "No, it wouldn't be enough." Execution, capital punishment, wouldn't completely satisfy me emotionally. If the offender were executed, he would be dying for something he did – he would deserve it.

Candace was innocent. She died young, in her prime, full of potential, full of anticipation, full of dreams – full of immediate plans for a good weekend. She would have contributed so much to our lives. Just to execute the offender would mean that he was being punished for what he had done. It would be removing a liability to society, a hopeless case. There's no equity in that. I was shocked at my own answer. But I continued, "His death, one death, wouldn't satisfy me...." I went deeper into myself, groping for the feeling of equity. "Ten child murderers would have to die." I paused, still groping for the satisfaction of justice.

The black cloud jumped into the living room and ran around, panting with excitement.

It was almost as if another voice answered for me, "And I would have to pull the trigger myself."

In my mind's eye, I saw ten hooded figures lined up against a brick wall. There was a gun in my hand and, immediately, I took advantage of the moment and aimed and pulled the trigger ten times. The figures fell one by one. The feeling was delicious. They deserved to die.

The feeling was delicious.

Yuk....

This was uncharacteristic.

I heard the black cloud's panting rapidly increase.

How do you forgive the murderer of your child? It shouldn't be easy – and it wasn't.

"I forgive," I said to myself again….

The black cloud began to shrink…. I had the power.

I could make peace with this huge rage – this menacing black cloud.

I glanced at my watch. It was 6:30 p.m. I drove up the hill, parked the car – took my government-issued photo ID and my social insurance card out of my wallet, stuck them into my coat, and locked my purse in the car.

René was already at the security desk. Well – he was on the other side of security – waiting nervously, as I knew he would be. I was processed quickly – much more quickly than usual.

Staff all seemed to be aware of René.

Then I went down the hallway. My eyes were on René, following him. I had no idea where we were going…. I expected to enter into the dome that would lead us to the prison cell area. Instead, we took a side door, a nondescript door, down a flight of stairs that opened to a large room.

My immediate response was that this was completely different than what one would expect in a prison. It didn't look like the official institutional offices, nor the prisoner cells.

It felt like a lounge – minus a well-supplied bar. There was a counter for coffee and refreshments in a room of chairs and sofas. Through the one door, I could see a pool table and through another, weights for training.

The mellow beige walls had been covered with dramatic murals, depicting violence. They were striking and beautiful.

Then along the walls – there were huge aquariums. Some had freshwater fish, others saltwater fish. When I asked about them, René told me that they were actually a business venture. The lifers would buy fish from outside stores and bring them in – raise them and sell them back to the retailers.

I was toured by René, some of the lifers, and the parole officers. I was told that this lifers' lounge was unique in all of Canada. It was opened as a privileged benefit to all the lifers who conformed to the prison expectations. Everyone was promised safety in this room – and everything in the room had been provided by the lifers themselves.

After the tour, I was invited to sit on a chair as the lifers sat down on the sofas and chairs around me.

That's when I noticed the parole officers leave through a side door – and I felt alone – very alone. They had been my guards. I was left guard-less.

René sat directly opposite – positioned himself so that he could see both my face and all the faces of the lifers.

He introduced me and reassured me that I was safe in that lifers' room – probably safer than I had ever been.

Then he gave a background history and orientation about the meeting.

"One time, I told Wilma that she needed to go to prison and talk to lifers. I said, 'You are asking me questions I cannot answer. I need to introduce you to people who have taken lives so that you can talk to them directly.' I was able to arrange a meeting.

"There is only one rule that I have made for those who wanted to attend."

Then the lifers took over – talking randomly, describing the room and their program.

They were proud of the lounge that they had created, decorated, and furnished.

They then described their organization – especially the peer support group where they would include the "new fish" – meaning the new lifers to the prison. They had a "buddy system" – guys to talk with when the rage became too much.

Then they said that "life" meant "life." They reassured me that even though they could apply for parole, not all of them did. They knew that they would never get out on the street – without being monitored and on parole.

Violation of any parole meant that they would be immediately sent back into prison. They talked a lot about the new law, 745 – the Faint Hope Clause – which was seen as giving freedom. It was a hot topic – very difficult to achieve – much less hope for.

Then René cleared his throat, and everyone turned to him. For me, it was very obvious that he was in complete charge of them. I couldn't help but remember his reputation in prison. I had no doubt that they were afraid of crossing him. I think that was when I realized that I was safe – at least physically safe.

Once he had their attention, René then turned the meeting over to me. "This is the one rule. You can ask any question you want from any one of the guys."

It was my turn to talk. That was when I felt uncomfortable, stalled. Two men were sitting behind me.

"I hope you don't mind," I started, "but I would really like these two gentlemen behind me to join the circle – where I can see them." I glanced at them.

There was a hush – a significant hush – a significant pause. I just waited. I was not going to talk with someone behind me.

I had no idea what I had just asked them to do.

Slowly – very slowly – they got up and moved their chairs into the circle. It was a big African American and his rather quiet sidekick.

The man sitting next to René smiled. "Thank you, guys! And I want to congratulate you, Wilma – not just anyone can move those guys."

The group broke into nervous laughter.

"I'm sorry, I just needed to see you," I said in a whisper. They nodded. I could tell they weren't happy – but they did not leave.

René said, "Now, let's start. Don't forget the rule. You can ask any question you want from any one of the guys."

I had my list of questions. My first was: What did you do? In other words, I was asking them for their prison ID. What were they in for? They said that it was generally against their code of anonymity in prison to respond, but they would do it for me.

I wondered if we could go around the circle…and if they would answer my simple, basic question. I wanted to know their sentence and how much time they had left. I asked them to explain to me what they did and what made them do it – to give me an explanation without making any excuses for themselves.

Sitting beside René was the president. He said he would start. The room was quiet. "Believe it or not, I am falsely accused. I didn't kill the man I was accused of killing."

"Then you aren't a lifer?" I asked. Thinking – this is great. Here I am with these convicted lifers, and they are all going to deny that they killed someone. It's going to be one huge denial – and what is the purpose of that?

"No, I'm not a lifer. But I am a member here because I was convicted of murder – and I have often wanted to kill someone. I understand killing. I understand these men. But I also understand you," he paused. "My father was murdered." And believe it or not, there was understanding in his eyes. We were all taken aback.

"Understand me?"

He nodded. It convinced me again that there is a fine line between victims and offenders. I didn't need any more of an explanation.

We carried on.

The next to speak was a young Indigenous man who said he had killed his common-law wife. He explained that he had come from a violent background, and thought he needed a gun to protect himself, and was surprised that he had used it in a rage.

Next to him was a man who said that when his partner abused and hurt his two-month-old daughter, he flew into a rage. He didn't know why – but in therapy realized that he had been abused as a child and was really killing all of those who had abused him. He couldn't make it out in the world – he was institutionalized. He deliberately drank so he could come back to prison to be in his comfort zone. He had been in prison for twenty-five years.

Next was a good-looking, young, Romeo-type man who said he had killed his wife in broad daylight – a brutal killing on a prominent street in Winnipeg – because he felt that his wife was making out with a friend.

Then there was an Asian man, with glasses, who said he had been suffering depression because his marriage of thirteen years had failed, and he had set fire to his in-law's house, badly burning the family – and killing one. He had been picked up by the police the very next day. Everyone knew....

Then there was an exceptionally friendly man with a small frame. He said that he was a survivor who had lived on the street and had fallen in with drug dealers to survive. He had entered into prison because of drugs. But once inside, he had fought to belong. When someone called him a goof, his honor was at stake and he killed the man. His second killing was in keeping with the first. He didn't know that he had options. He didn't know that he could walk away from an insult.

The next was a balding, American soldier-type. He said that he had killed his best friend when they had fought over a woman in a bar. There had never been any intention to kill, but the anger had escalated so that when his friend pulled out a weapon, he killed his friend in self-defense. It probably could have been a tossup as to who would have been killed – he had just been the better fighter because of his training in the army.

Then there was an African American man – the one who had not wanted to sit in the circle. He said that he couldn't look at himself for six months after he had killed a man – except to wash his face. He was in because of a drug-related killing. He said that he was too proud to commit suicide so he hurt and killed others instead.

Then there was a studious-looking man who said that his entire family were teachers, and he had never fit in. It was a strong, patriarchal family where everyone was assumed to be strong. Keep the family happy and never show anger. He hadn't been strong. He had never shown any anger – and then he had, in a fit of rage, killed his wife.

As they talked, I noticed that the black cloud beside me was quietly listening with me. Why, I wondered? Was it intimidated – as I was?

At the beginning, I had told them that I couldn't listen to murder being excused, rationalized, or minimized, especially justified. I had learned that if I heard murder being minimized, it triggered me. The story of the apology needed to match the story of the crime. There needs to be harmony between them. The truth of it – ownership of and responsibility for the crime – needed to match the gravity of the crime.

They were able to do this.

Here in the Lifers' Lounge, it seemed as if the black clouds remained separated – shackled to their individual owner. It was interesting that some black clouds dominated the owner; some owners dominated their black cloud.

These were the same nocturnal apparitions that haunted our survivors support group.

Except these vicious, black clouds seemed to be more comfortable here – more attached to their owners. They were in control. They had defeated their owners.

In that one moment when they had turned their owners – calm, rational, thinking individuals – into wild animals – irrational, out of control with murderous, dangerous intentions – the black clouds had taken over. They had won. Their owners had turned into killers.

This was compounded by the fact that these men were on the other side of the law. Society as a whole, media and friends, had all but forsaken them. They were annihilated. There was no way out for these men. They smelt of death.

The black clouds had them.

Then I simply asked some more questions: What did/do you wish out of life? What would you need to heal?

As we were closing down, I asked them how they felt.

It wasn't hard for them to answer. "Humiliated."

Some said, "Ashamed."

I felt their pain.

I thanked them profusely and expected to be escorted out.

But the man opposite me – the president – said, "Now it's your turn. We want to hear your story and what you think."

I then briefly told my story as I always did – this time without notes.

They listened intently.

Then they asked me, "What do victims want?"

"To feel safe," I replied. "To have an explanation."

"Why do they want to know so badly?"

I was surprised that they didn't know why victims wanted to know every detail…obsessively so.

It was hard to explain to them. Victims need to make sense of the violence, yet this information is not accessible. It was true, they will often begin a fact-finding journey and truth-telling quest to find the answers to the violence they have just experienced. They might insist on seeing the medical examiner's report, talk to everyone who was part of the crime, meet other survivors or read books on violence and crime.

It was complicated when the victims' "need to know" conflicted with their natural desire to avoid anything that was frightening, horrifying, or painful. This was also a weird kind of "stuckness."

But I couldn't say all that. I said simply, "They want to know who is responsible – who to blame. If we can't find an 'other' to blame, we will blame ourselves."

That they understood….

They then took the time to reassure me that they would change with time – and with their programs.

"Do you believe in face-to-face programs?" they asked me.

"Yes," I replied.

I had a new qualification – it had to be safe.

By the end, we were all talking. The walls had been torn down, and we were freely discussing with each other – our doubts, our questions, our shame, our wishes, our dreams and our frustrations.

It became like every other group that dares to become real. It felt like just another self-help support group. It felt familiar – and yes – it even felt safe.

As I was driving home, I felt that something had shifted in me. Something big. My world would never be the same. I had seen the enemy, and he had looked like any other person on the street. The lifers were human beings.

I also realized, as I counted them in my mind, that there had been ten men in the room, including René – men who had killed, men who had wanted to kill, and men who had tried but failed. There had, in essence, been ten lifers in the room.

A long time ago – eleven years before – I had admitted to wanting to avenge Candace's death and kill ten murderers – now I had met them. I had sat with ten violent men, eight who admitted to being killers, and I had not wanted to kill any of them.

In fact, I had felt something akin to compassion.

PART II

Chapter 13
STORM

Everything changed after the meeting with the lifers at Stony Mountain.

I still had those small clouds filled with memories, emotions, sadness and grief – but the presence of that fierce, funneling wind was gone. I hadn't even realized how much wind there was in those reptilian clouds.

Released from the encumbering clouds meant that I wasn't a victim advocate much anymore and was free to pursue other things.

For some irrational reason I thought I would go into Real Estate, for the simple reason that I loved fixing up old houses.

In very short order, I took a real estate course, received my license, found a wonderful partner, and landed my first potential sale.

It was a little house in my area that was being sold by an elderly couple moving into an independent living community. This was their first step in downsizing.

I sensed their grief, their anguish, and their fears as we set up the parameters of that first showing.

They wanted to be present – actually, there was no place for them to go – so when a promising buyer came through the door, we were all very optimistic.

He was a middle-aged man who asked all the right questions as we toured the first floor. When that was completed, we went into the basement....

It was unfinished for the most part...dark...but with no evidence of water damage. It was a viable basement – a perfect place for storage. I was pointing out all the best-selling features when the man cleared his throat.

"By the way...." He looked directly at me, excluding the owners very deliberately in his body language and the focus of his eyes. "I haven't come to buy a house."

Out of the corner of my eye, I could see the startled reaction of the owners of the house – instant alarm.

The man continued. "I've come to see you," he said, holding my eyes with an astonishing fierceness.

I was confused. "Me?"

"Yes – my daughter was murdered too."

Wrong place. Wrong time.

I glanced at the owners – their eyes were huge.

"Who are you?" they asked me.

The stranger told them that I wasn't really a realtor, I was the mother of a murdered child, Candace. Everyone knew Candace, he said. Everyone knew the story of her murder.

The owners' eyes grew even larger now that they recognized me from the news broadcasts.

I broke the moment by quickly making an appointment with him to meet at another time, in another place, at a coffee shop, as I ushered him out.

I then turned to console the disappointed owners – promising them that I had a very reliable, capable partner who would be in contact with them shortly for another showing.

Leaving them, I went home and resigned as a real estate broker and ended my partnership abruptly. I knew I couldn't continue – I attracted all the wrong people.

Worse yet, I had put vulnerable people at risk.

For the next few days, I just hid in our house, rethinking it all.

It was probably the first time I had stepped off the treadmill of life since Candace's murder to take stock of what I was doing and who I was.

I resented the man who pretended to be a potential buyer, the man who had experienced murder in his family. I had lost my compassion. I never did call him.

Would I never escape this victim identity? I was filled with self-pity.

Cliff was floundering too. He had resigned from his work at Camp Arnes. He was great with children and a natural teacher, but with the suspicions around our family – the unspoken wonderings of whether he had taken Candace that night – though never tangible or spoken – seemed to be taking their toll. He wasn't a good face for any organization anymore. It was cruel to watch him being sidelined again and again. Finally, he isolated himself. Resigned from it all. We were truly drifting.

Odia was now a young adult – moving out of our home to live with roommates. She had survived her tumultuous teen years and had emerged a very sensible young woman. An artist like her father, she was taking Fine Arts at the University of Manitoba and doing well.

Syras was fourteen years old, in high school – and he had proven to be an adult child right from the beginning, with a maturity far beyond his years. He was more together and responsible at fourteen than any of us would ever be. No worries there.

We were all into the arts. Three years after Candace was murdered, we moved to a house on Hazel Dell. We were all into pottery. We had a wheel in the basement…and Cliff was finding a new medium. Both Odia and Syras excelled on the wheel.

Then we hit a new low when we had a car accident that put Cliff in the hospital. Cliff was in dire shape.

I remember coming home from the hospital, noticing that our house was a shambles. We were renovating this older house – and it seemed to be always in a state of chaos. I never did like the house – there was no chemistry.

When Cliff was out of the hospital, both of us – usually law-abiding, conscientious drivers – were racking up speeding tickets.

Cliff, at one point, was threatened with a driving suspension. We were becoming unhinged again – reckless. Angry at everything.

Even our children looked at us in bewilderment. "Are you running away from God?" they asked. "Are you Jonah?" they asked, referring to the well-known Bible story of a man who ran away from God when asked to go to Nineveh – the man who had been swallowed by a big fish and changed his mind. When Jonah capitulated, the big fish spit him onto shore so that he could return to the city of Nineveh where he fulfilled God's wishes.

That word, Jonah, was laden with all kinds of meanings. Were we running away from God? That would explain the wild storm – the feeling of being trapped – the suffocation – the desperation – the nausea.

We took stock of our lives. Cliff started on his journey of healing by memorizing the Book of Jonah and was able to recite the whole book in twelve minutes.

I too had to examine my life.

What was I running away from?

After ten years in my position as Western Regional Editor of the *Mennonite Reporter* my time with them was over. I had covered enough stories of church dysfunction, church authority figures caught in sexual sin – conference politics – that I was left suspicious of the organized church and its leaders. My faith in God was still intact – but my faith in the church was wavering.

After seven years of working with the survivors support group, I had lost my enthusiasm for my program with victims. I had used the group to gather my *Fifteen Elements*, organize them, present them to many others, have them validated – and I was tired of them as a support group – burned out. If I was honest, I felt rejected by them. I knew that they had never accepted my position on forgiveness and were using me as much as I was using them.

So I resigned from the *Mennonite Reporter*, and I closed the survivors support group program – against the wishes of the members. I claimed it was lack of money – which it was – but I was also relieved.

But now I was at sea – thrown overboard – drowning.

What was my Nineveh?

Jonah had an unwanted message to bring to Nineveh. Did I have a message?

Perhaps I did. I had found great healing in telling my story. And people seemed to want my story.

For example, just that August, I had been one of the plenary speakers, telling my story at The International Prison Chaplains Association held in Ottawa, hosted by Rev. Pierre Allard. In October, I had visited the McMaster Divinity College Conference in Hamilton, Ontario, and spoken on a victim's perspective of reconciliation.

In November, I had spoken to a Criminology Class on "Fifteen Elements of Healing," in Selkirk, Manitoba. In January, I had visited a prison, the Rockwood Institution, attending a banquet for inmates, speaking on "Fifteen Elements of Healing." The same month I had been on the CJOB radio show, talking about the "Role of Forgiveness." Then I had traveled to Prince Edward Island and attended the National Crime Prevention Conference in 1996 at the School of Justice, that included the police, victim services – to again tell the story of the "Fifteen Elements of Healing."

Even though I didn't relish the speaking in public, I found healing and fulfillment in the telling of my story to an appreciative audience.

I also recognized that I had a unique position as a parent of a murdered child. I had an acceptable victim story.

Even René, who had been in the Criminal Justice System for a lot longer than I, said that I was perfectly positioned to work with victims and offenders. He said that Candace was the perfect example of an innocent victim. At thirteen years of age, she had lived just long enough to know who she was and she had died before she could make any real mistakes.

He then added, "Because your case has remained unsolved, you are caught in a never-ending story of victimization." He had seen other crime victims lose interest in the system once their case had gone through the system. Apparently, we would never have that luxury. We were stuck, he said.

He was right. Now ten years later – even though we had moved beyond the initial grief and had come to some understanding of our black cloud and the one that growled – we were still caught in this victim world.

The first late-night visitor with that humongous, black cloud had been right – our lives would never be the same. We would never fit into society again in the same way.

Yet I wasn't comfortable in either the victim community or the criminal community. The victim community did not appreciate my attitude of forgiveness; the criminal community remained suspicious of my victim anger.

Where then was my Nineveh?

How could I get this angry God off my back, and get out of this fish's stomach?

Then it dawned on me.

There was only one organization that had been interested in cultivating my story – Mennonite Central Committee.

I called the director of a national restorative justice program.

And the minute I called, I felt a peace. This was the first sign that I might have appeased the storm.

The director just happened to be in town for some organizational meetings – that was the second sign.

And yes – he would love to meet with me. Could I meet him for breakfast the next day?

I took a deep breath. OK – this was fast. This was the third sign. Things were falling into place – too fast for me to ignore.

We met. I asked him if he had any need for a token victim in his program. They had used me a couple of times before – so I was just wondering.

He eyed me, studied me for a moment. "If you had a position with us, what would you do?" he asked.

I hadn't expected this question – I had thought he would know what a national program might need.

I looked through my purse for paper to write on. He gave me a napkin. I looked at it for a second, allowing myself to sink down deep into my soul and imagine myself able to do whatever I wanted to do to help crime victims deal with their black cloud.

Suddenly it was exciting. This was the fourth sign.

I started to write and dream, as I wrote. If I had my druthers as a victim myself, I would like an outlet to tell my story over and over again, in group support meetings, and in various publications. I would want a guided tour through the criminal justice processes. For a guide, I would want someone loyal to me, yet who was respected by the systems. I would want access to the offender if I needed it – again with a guide – my guide. I would want society as a whole to understand the complications of the role of the victim. I would want some validation, victim awareness and appreciation that would eventually curtail the uninformed stigmatization.

Here I stopped. Even the label "victim" was a problem. Many crime victims refused to label themselves as such, and I completely understood them. There is no social equity in the word "victim."

However, there should be. In the system, victimization was already gaining some attention. If I had my wish, there would be more. Victims should have a front seat in the drama played out on their lives. They should earn respect by this designation – not disrespect.

I was mumbling as I was writing.

And he was nodding.

"Would you take this on as a volunteer position?"

I gulped.

This was the true test of my idea that money might be the answer – a way to escape. A volunteer position meant that they would pay only a small honorarium for the first two years – and then, only if the program proved its value, would I be hired as full-time employee.

Did I have a choice?

Was this my new calling? There had been those four signs…. I smiled. And gave him the napkin. "Sure."

He smiled and stuffed it in his pocket.

"When can you start?"

"September," I said.

I really didn't think I would hear from him again. No one would accept my naïve proposal.

But at the very least, I had appeased my God.

Shortly after that I was hired and moved into an office at Mennonite Central Committee Winnipeg, tasked with the ominous responsibility as Director of Victims' Voice – a new program.

All the time I was doing this, I was very aware that this really wasn't what I wanted to do with my life – even though it was what I thought victims would need – what I would have needed. And I could feel the excitement of creating the program, but not in the position. I was conflicted.

As a child I would never have wanted to be a director of a victims' program. This was not my dream job – and never my aspiration. Even real estate had not been my first choice.

And I knew it would be very difficult to work with a group of people, secondary victims of homicide, who were always suspicious of me. Right from the beginning, this group had told me to "lose the word forgiveness" and I hadn't said it for seven years. Yet I had lived it – even brought them along with me on some of my forgiveness ventures – yet the tension remained. The tension had burned me out once – could I endure it a second time? I was worried.

In sorting through a box of children's toys I found a little lamb. It was just a tiny farm ornament, but suddenly I identified with the little lamb. Submission, sacrifice. It was the only thing between me and the big blue sea.

I took it into the office that first day and put it on my desk.

My first assignment was to produce a Victims' Voice Mission Statement.

I had a great internal struggle to think this through. My natural inclination was to base the program on the word "forgiveness." It would have been so natural and easy for me. But I knew MCC – even though it was faith based – wasn't driven by faith language. It was based solely on helping others wherever they were. They would not wish me to force forgiveness language on anyone. Which I agreed with. I had seen what that message of forgiveness had done to the victim community – it had devastated them. I too had been uncomfortable when anyone had said, "Just forgive."

In many ways itemizing those fifteen elements was my protest to everyone. I was saying, "It is not that easy to forgive. It is more than just hanging around a church. It's a comprehensive lifestyle change."

On the other hand, if I didn't declare my forgiveness stance publicly, was I denying the victim community that choice and even more importantly – denying my faith?

That's when I remembered the Samaritan Story.

The parable of the Good Samaritan is about a traveler who is stripped of his clothing, beaten, and left half dead alongside the road. Two men of faith come across him, but both avoid the man. Finally, a marginalized Samaritan happens upon the traveler.

The Samaritan both felt and showed compassion towards the beaten man. He used wine and oil – expensive goods – to tend to the man's wounds, took him to an inn, paid in advance for two days of care, and offered to pay more as needed, with no assurance of receiving anything in return.

There are two significant messages. Love breaks social boundaries with practical help. Crime victims don't need only justice – they need help and time to heal. They need others to help them. Secondly, crime victims need to be taken to an inn. They need a place of their own that would give them the comfort and time to heal.

For me this parable also showed that the victim comes first. The story did not say that the authority figures should have gone after the offender to rehabilitate him. The traveler beside the road, unjustly beaten, was the victim at hand. He was the first priority.

This was very important in my work. In a federal offense, if the offender is put first, healing does not happen. In a serious crime like murder, the victims need to come first for there to be any hope of a satisfying justice.

For me this parable also clarified the place of faith and church organizations and their role in social justice issues. They are often too preoccupied with organizational duties to look after the travelers. That responsibility lies with the people who understand – and are of like experience.

The Samaritan, by his very status in society, would have understood victimization.

I had my marching orders – I understood. I understood the victim community.

This was reflected in my mandate.

In realization of the need for hurting victims to be united under a common goal of hope and healing Victims' Voice is a non-profit, national program providing member victims of serious crime with a safe place to connect with each other, with their community and with other healing services that will enable them to become functioning and contributing members of society again.

My second task was to create a national victim awareness.

From the fall of 1996 to the spring of 1998, I crisscrossed the country – even dipping into the States – to speak.

I would enter into a small town and do multiple presentations. I spent three days in one town and presented fifteen times. For example, in Kamloops, I found myself speaking at a homeless center, to first responders, correctional services and women's outreach. In the same town, I addressed students in a Christian school, the pastors of the community in a ministerial, and two churches, extremely different from each other. Oh yes – and I was also on the radio. I sometimes felt I was in perpetual culture shock.

I was also doing a juggling act – assessing each audience and trying to adapt to their needs – whatever I guessed them to be. I found that each time my stories were somewhat different. I was growing and moving.

For the churches, I preached, "And now these three remain: faith, hope and love. But the greatest of these is love."

For the others, I spoke on my *Fifteen Elements* – racing through them, abbreviating them for a twenty-minute or an hour-long presentation – always selecting a few elements and telling bits of my story.

In each presentation, I would always start with the stranger coming and us choosing forgiveness and love – a counter-intuitive choice that led us on a winding path through trauma embedded with fifteen issues. I would always include my story of wanting to personally execute the ten child murderers. It was always personal.

I always came home exhausted.

Only to go on the road again to another town. During one week, I spoke twice in Vancouver – had a moment to touch the Pacific Ocean – and then flew to St. John's, Newfoundland, where I touched the Atlantic Ocean, and spoke seven times to various organizations. And then I headed up to Happy Valley-Goose Bay, Labrador, where I spoke thirteen times.

It was like an educational tour of the country. I wasn't only presenting; I was also listening.

I was always in the presence of the clouds – either in the audience or near me when I told my story.

In Labrador – during a presentation – one gentleman at the back of the room asked me, "Do you think perhaps those fifteen elements could apply to our community?"

"Yes," I said and then, along with him and the audience, we went through the *Fifteen Elements* again. This time they offered the application. They concluded. "Yes, our story was broken. We were traumatized with fear. We lost our identity." We continued through all the fifteen until, together, we hit the last one.

One hundred percent of the people who lose their child to homicide do contemplate suicide. We paused. They nodded. Suicide haunted their community.

Another memorable moment was when I was speaking in a well-established church in a Mennonite community. In these churches, I didn't really preach a sermon. I was just asked to tell my story. Somehow, I was allowed to speak from the pulpit that Sunday morning.

Then, as was their custom, the pastor asked me to stand at the front door and greet all the members as they left the sanctuary.

This meant I shook hands with everyone in the congregation – and connected with them for only a minute.

That moment was enough. I don't know what I said in my story that prompted this, but as they would take my hand, they leaned closer and whispered in my ear – so no one else could hear them – little glimpses into their lives. "My husband beats me." "I was molested by my uncle." "I was assaulted." "I was raped by my cousin." "I was arrested." "I am desperate for justice. My sister was killed." "I'm suffering from depression." "My husband was killed…."

It was a staccato glimpse of every possible abusive situation – every cloud. One would never have suspected this in such a rich, prominent church – but there it was. They would whisper it in my ear, then turn and leave – walk out the door and down the stairs to their cars….

I was reeling.

I remember just wanting to scream. Stop! You can't just tell me this and walk out. We need to stop this! I went back to my hotel room and sobbed.

There was another audience in Vancouver – it was filled with victim service workers and police officers. Professionals.

Halfway into my presentation, I noticed that there was a man sitting in the third row that was staring at me – viciously. His eyes were glaring – glazed with unspeakable anger.

I was really nervous when I had finished, and saw him come towards me. He stood patiently in line to talk to me. I tried to draw out the conversations of the others in the hopes that he would get tired and leave as I was trying hard to concentrate on everyone telling me their stories, trying to respond appropriately.

But when his time came, instead of giving me a tongue-lashing as I expected, he grabbed my hand tenderly. "You are amazing," he said softly. "You almost make me cry." There were lingering tears in his eyes. I think I gave him a hug.

I tried not to giggle. What do I know about facial expressions? I decided never to trust my "reading of an audience" again.

As the demand for my speaking increased, the MCC program director grew excited. Along with many in the restorative justice movement, she believed that story was important in creating change.

I believed it as well. I had seen it. Story accesses our emotions, and therefore is important to decision-making. It creates meaning out of experiences. It gives a sense of belonging. It engenders empathy and sympathy across differences. It surpasses our rational minds and allows us to dream. When it comes to change, story is foundational.

We decided to produce a newsletter of hope and healing for victims of violent crime. It had a yellow theme, for light and "making lemonade out of lemons." We called it *Pathways*. Each issue profiled the story of a murder, highlighting a victim who had dealt with it uniquely.

The main purpose of each issue was to explore one of the *Fifteen Elements*.

I would analyze the element, explore it from many different angles, memorialize the loved ones murdered, suggest readings, and connections. We also had guest columnists.

Part of dissecting the element was the need to find solutions. For example, the first element we talked about was Story Fragmentation.... This led to encourage the telling of story – completing the story, having the story validated and then recreating the story – entering into it to change the course of the story. There were no formulas; we all had to do it differently but the elements helped organize the conversations.

My travel across the country gave me access to the victims' stories that I wanted to pursue – stories I could identify with. They were all victims who were proactive about their lot in life – making choices to fight through the aftermath of murder rather than succumb to trauma.

In September 1998 – I came out with my first story about Jake Plett, who had written a book, *Valley of Shadows,* a true account of his wife, Mary Ann – a real estate agent who had gone to show a house to a client and had never returned. They found her body seven months later.

He had come to visit us during a book tour when Cliff and I lived in North Battleford. I was impressed with his pearls of wisdom – and his outlook on his life and his tragedy. It influenced me – impressed me so much that when Candace disappeared, I pulled out his book and lived by his philosophy. He was a guiding light.

Unfortunately, by the time I wanted to talk to him again, he had died in an airplane crash, so I sought out his two sons, who were images of him. They confirmed for me that what we live will show itself in our children. They were amazing – and made for an amazing first edition.

I remember calling Carol Pearce, who was also a mentor of mine. Here in Manitoba, her story of forgiveness is legendary.

It was in 1976 that her husband had been killed during a home invasion.

The stories were vivid but, looking over the editions, I realize the pictures are always fuzzy. I like out of focus. That was another distinction of ours, we loved our fuzzy photos – at least I did.

After covering the *Fifteen Elements*, I ended *Pathways* in 2001. In September 2001 we all experienced 9/11 – an event where the entire world went through the fifteen elements.

And I was now ready to write the book. In 2002, I published *Confronting the Horror, the Aftermath of Violence* – a textbook outlining the fifteen elements of trauma. It was never a bestseller – but it was important to my work. We also wrote *Getting through the Maze: a Guidebook for Survivors of Homicide*, and other publications.

Writing like this and storytelling was fulfilling! I could have done this forever!

In the meantime – I never forgot my real agenda which was to heal the victims' hearts. Not to placate them, silence them, or use them, but to drill down into the real issues, to try to solve their presenting problems, and give their lives meaning again. It was even more than just helping them with their stories or describing the fifteen-step journey. It was much bigger than that.

My real mandate was to design a program which would help crime victims move through their grief journey and not get stuck. That was the dreaded word. And they would often get stuck in their trauma clouds of anger, fear and complex grief.

As far as I knew, the only way to deal with their trauma cloud was to attend support groups, so I decided to revive the survivors support group. It worked.

I'll never forget one group meeting when we were visited by the husband of one of the members. She hadn't been able to come so he had decided to come.

He came in, dark cloud first. In fact, for the first half hour that's all we could see as he blasted us in the group. "You are accomplishing nothing!" he ranted. "You are pathetic – just sitting here in this rundown church telling your stories, crying and feeling sorry for yourselves. You need to be doing something!" His trauma cloud was fierce!

At this point, we didn't even hear his offensive words being hurled at us. All we saw was the thunder and lightning of his cloud. Frightening really. What did he expect us to do?

He didn't put it in words, but we suspected that he wanted us to kill a few murderers, such as the man who had killed his son, and throw a few politicians and judges out of their honored positions, shaming everyone in the system.

It felt violating.

His eyes were blazing.

He tired after a while – and all I could see was the pain that was left in his eyes.

Then we asked him about the murder and loss of his son. He began to tell his story. At first it was an angry story – then a beautiful story and finally it was choked with all kinds of emotion. He ended it in a puddle of tears. Man tears. Wrenched out with pain and disgust, but vulnerable just the same.

We all just sat there – with shocked fascination at the display of this magnificent thunderstorm – roaring into our midst, putting on an impressive display of power but then dissipating into the soft shower of nourishing, life-giving, healing rain.

He left – his eyes shining. Hugging us and telling us it was the best group support meeting ever. None of us really could fathom or believe the miracle we had seen in him – we kind of just put it out of our minds.

But it was confirmed by his wife who returned to us – thanking us for what we had accomplished with her husband. "He truly is a changed man. He said you were the best," she told us over and over again.

Years later when I met him again – he grasped my hand with the same glow in his eyes that I had seen that evening.

Tears – we underestimate the healing power of tears.

As I reflected on the group – if there was any consistent program agenda that was healing – it was the tears. We would come into the meeting, angry – and tell our stories till someone brought us to tears. Then we would cry and go home happy. It wasn't as simple as that – but it almost was.

And we encouraged each other to cry every day. We all agreed that the best time to cry was during that alone moment between the day at the office and meeting the family at home. It was part of the evening's agenda – how did you induce the tears this week?

Did it work? Sometimes I wish we would have had a research team study our group because, anecdotally, I think I could say it worked.

We became even more aware of the power of tears when a victims' group leader from another province come to observe our group. She commented on the tears. Then in a debrief after, she shared that one of the biggest problems with her support group back home was the growing percentage of divorces that were threatening the cohesion of the group. She wondered what we did with all the divorces.

I had to think – we hadn't experienced any members divorcing. Their marriages weren't the best – but no divorces. I wondered about the power of grieving tears to heal....

But there was one more problem in the healing process of victimization, it can't be just emotional support. We do need to address the Criminal Justice System.

We needed to learn to work with the system.

To learn more about this, I organized an advisory of victim service workers in Winnipeg.

If we were ever able to develop our ideal, custom-designed victim program, we would have to include a good working relationship with those on the frontlines.

Around this time, I saw that little lamb ornament still sitting on my desk and I dropped it into the toy box again. I had no need of it. I was enjoying this…something I would never have expected in a million years.

I had finally embraced my identity of being the parent of a murdered child.

Chapter 14
SURROGATE

However, it still wasn't enough. Three years into the program, I knew I had to address the victim-offender trauma bond again.

I remembered the encounters, the letter, the hundred inmates, the Lifers' Lounge. I had learned something important in these encounters.

When the trauma cloud of a crime victim encounters the aggressive, hostile cloud of a criminal, they both become very territorial. There isn't much difference in the clouds on either side. They are all murky – inky, revolting clouds, teeming with all kinds of unhealthy emotions, creating winds of aggression.

Yet, when a victim cloud senses a perceived enemy cloud, it is triggered – quickly and explosively. It can turn from a wisp of a wind into a threatening tornado at a moment's notice.

I've seen victims – good people – turn into revengeful clouds threatening to demolish everyone – if not physically, then emotionally.

I've also seen criminals with a history of violence, when vulnerable, reveal a hidden victim cloud inside, cohabitating with the offender cloud – both clouds embracing the same feelings of self-pity and hatred.

Yet, bring a victim cloud and an offender cloud together, and there is potential for huge learning as they recognize their issues in the dysfunction of the other. It can be like chemotherapy – a shock that brings healing – or if not handled correctly, they can destroy each other.

When it is good, it is very good – when it goes wrong, it is ugly.

We needed to nail it down – master it.

I needed to try this again in a safe place. There was much more to learn.

It was time – three years into the program as Director of Victims' Voice.

I called René.

He was sitting at a table near the windows, waiting for me. He folded up his newspaper when I slid into the booth opposite him. I could tell that he had come early – very early. At least that hadn't changed. He was always early.

"Morning, René," I said, ordering coffee and toast. He did the same. "How are you doing?"

I hadn't seen him for three years.

"Good – and you?" he asked.

"Lots has changed." I felt I had changed. The last time I had seen him had been in the Lifers' Lounge – when I had felt desperate and alone. Since then, I had traveled the world, it seemed, and discovered that my experience was more widespread than I thought. I had fresh ideas as to how important the victim-offender encounters could be.

He nodded, glancing around the restaurant. "We are in a new restaurant? Do you work around here?" This time when I had called him I had invited him to meet at Perkins on the corner of Bishop Grandin and Pembina.

I nodded.

Then he waited. That's when I noticed his watchfulness. I knew he was curious and could have asked a million questions, but he didn't. He had never, ever overstepped or pushed in any way. He never probed. He would wait patiently for my lead.

There was no time to waste. "I wanted to check up – find out where you are at – because I have a favor to ask."

"Whatever you ask...," he said.

"As you know, the organization that I'm now working for is exploring Restorative Justice."

He nodded.

"To do that, I will need someone who knows the prison world."

He nodded. "I will help you in whatever way I can."

Perfect. I had what I wanted.

Now for the job interview.

"Tell me again, exactly what it is that you do in prison," I said, taking a sip of my coffee.

He might not be a great, empathic listener with his guarded eyes – but as a storyteller, all guards were down – and he would live his stories.

He began…. "About four years ago, I was asked by the Stony Mountain warden to start the Life Line Program. It was a program for people who had murdered someone, so there was some resistance to my being hired because I wasn't in prison for murder. I was violent – but I wasn't a murderer. Then two years after that, I became an Inreach Worker for Life Line."

"Then, that was an easy fit…."

He paused. "Well, actually, they didn't think so – not at first – at least."

"It was because of the warden at the time. He said, 'If you want Life Line in my prison, I'll tell you who you will hire. René is the only guy I can trust to come back into my jail. If you don't hire him, we'll just walk away from the program.' That was very powerful for the warden to say that. But the warden had seen the way I worked with the groups inside. I had kicked some people out of groups because they were trying to play games with me. I was a straight shooter in prison. I would say to the guys in all the groups, 'If you don't like it, come and see me.' There aren't too many people who can do that in prison. Three or four months later, the warden called me back and said, 'René, there is a possible job opening at Stony for Life Line.'

"This was a pretty great validation of what I was doing from the warden, who had helped me to be released. It was a huge encouragement to me to keep on the path that I had started in jail, turning my life around.

"Finally, the founding members of the Life Line organization came to Stony, and we met there. It was agreed that I would be the next Life Line worker for Stony Mountain and Rockwood.

"My first task was to go to Kingston and spend a week with Tom French, and he provided me with the training for the job. For me, it was the right position from the start. I believed so strongly in that program. It is as if the program was designed exactly for a guy like me.

"In fact, I said to Tom, 'You know what? I am always going to appreciate the training you have provided for me. But there are some things I just know because I've been on the inside. I, as an inmate, am particularly suited to help my fellow inmates to see the truth about their life, to see the impact of their crime. Because I've changed, I can also help them to try to change their life.'

"After the training, I came back to Winnipeg, and I began to work at Stony Mountain Institution.

"When I started, I was so committed I worked around the clock. I was in prison twelve or thirteen hours a day. The warden once said, 'René, get the hell out of here. You have to take time with your family.' But for me, it was not just a job, it was like a mission. I saw myself as a merchant of hope.

"Even when I went home, everything was set up to work from home. I had my computer at home and a telephone system that allowed me to hook up with the inmates at a moment's notice. I let them all know that if they were desperate – to call me before they did something wrong. I told that to every one of my clients. 'Call me any time of the night.' I had permission from the warden to hand out my telephone number on all the ranges. Every inmate could call me on an 800 number because I was the last line of defense, if I can use that term.

"Lots of these guys who gave up on life were really dangerous to themselves and others. So, for me, I wanted to let them know that I was available. I begged them, 'Give me a chance to talk to you. If you want to do something, I will not stop you. Just give me a chance to talk to you and, if I can't help you, I will let you go and do what you want.'

"But I knew that if I could get the fellow into my office, he would never get out of there before I was finished with him the way I wanted him to be. No one ever did anything drastic after spending one hour, five hours, or whatever with me. The time didn't matter. I spent whatever time I needed with a guy to make sure he was okay."

Then he paused. "What do you want me to do?"

I shoved the cutlery aside and laid down my notebook. This time I had a concrete, complicated assignment for which I needed his help.

"I asked you out for breakfast because I have another project." I took a breath. This was so exciting. "I would like to set up our first encounter. Much like the one you did with me. This time two women want to go into Stony Mountain to meet inmates. They feel stuck and heard of our previous surrogate encounters."

He nodded. "Who are they? What crimes?"

I briefly described the two cases – one was the murder of a brother, the other the murder of a daughter in a domestic dispute. Both felt stuck in their anger. Both had expressed an interest in a surrogate encounter.

"Do I know them?"

"Laura and Lynne…."

He went a little pale…. "I know Lynne…."

"How do you know her?"

"She is French," he paused. "She grew up with Suzanne…." His voice trailed away.

"Is this a problem?"

"Yes. It might be – not for me – but for Lynne. She knows about how I hurt Suzanne. She knows about my double life and how often I betrayed Suzanne."

He shook his head with regret. "I betrayed her so often. Even after we were married, I betrayed her. Suzanne didn't know when I robbed department stores. She was never even aware. If she had known, it would have been the end – the end of everything. I did things and always managed to hide them from her. I never deposited the money in a bank account. I just told her, 'I got a job for a couple of days.' I always had cash. I didn't even have a bank account. It's easy to keep the money if you have only $5,000 or so. You can keep it in your pockets. She trusted me. She would never have thought in a million years that I would rob that department store. It's always easy to hide something from someone who loves you and wants to believe in you. She loved me and wanted to believe in me. When it was discovered later on how I had betrayed her – Suzanne would talk to her friends. They hated me for hurting Suzanne."

He shrugged. "I don't blame them."

I realized again the complexity of working with someone who had been a career criminal.

"Would Suzanne mind this – you facilitating a conversation for Lynne?" I asked.

He shrugged again. "No, she doesn't mind. Her friends might."

"I will ask Lynne."

He nodded.

The next day when I met Lynne – it was exactly as he predicted. She was still angry with René. "He hurt Suzanne…. He's an asshole."

"Should we call it off?" I asked.

She looked long and hard at me as I waited. I couldn't imagine what she was processing – all those talks with Suzanne – having to face all of those friendship issues.

"I guess I have to accept it – this is about learning about criminals." There was another long pause. "Yes, I will do it."

Who would have thought that the process of dealing with the offender would begin with René and Lynne?

We set a date.

Everything was going well until the heavy prison doors clanged shut behind us, and we were walking through the corridors toward the room to meet with the inmates.

Lynne started to shake. Of the two women coming with me, I had thought Lynne would be the leader – strong, expressive, and outspoken.

But something suddenly had changed. She seemed very nervous – unusually nervous.

That's when I realized the black clouds were there in full force.

She was starting to shake. I was trying to reassure her that she had nothing to fear, but it wasn't helping – yet she would not turn around and leave.

Just before we were about to enter the lounge, she wilted completely – sinking into the chair and just sobbing. Nothing seemed to comfort her. We were helpless.

Finally, I asked again. "Should we leave? We don't have to do this," I said – reassuring her over and over again.

All the time I was wondering how I could have prepared her better. I should have known – people change in prison. The black clouds are overwhelming.

Slowly – very slowly, she gained control over herself, and we walked in.

The room had been set up the way we requested. We were at one end of the table, the men at the other. There was no contact.

René welcomed them in…. "Do whatever you want, and don't do anything you don't want to do."

We reassured the two victims over and over again. "Whatever you want – just tell me. These guys are willing to take whatever you have."

Once they were seated, I introduced the two victim storytellers. René introduced the four inmates. We did a bit of chitchat, which never works. No one cares about the weather outside.

Then I told my story briefly to break the tenseness. The fellows had heard it all before and nodded politely.

Then I turned to Lynne and asked if she wanted to begin.

She took a deep breath, and the tears – so near the surface – began to stream down her cheeks again.

"Losing a family member has got to be the worst thing that can ever happen to anybody. When somebody kills somebody, they just don't kill the person that dies, they kill the whole family."

Her face was flushed, as she began to rage.

"When a person is murdered, everybody goes away from the family. You don't have friends anymore because they don't know what to say. The friends who do stay can turn vindictive. I don't know why they have to be so mean. We didn't do anything wrong."

She gulped and looked down. "My brother's murderer was acquitted and lives as a free man in the States. So, while he's enjoying his life, we are picking up the pieces, and our hearts die inch by inch every day."

She was quiet for a long while.

I wanted to take her hand but resisted. It takes the person's power away. I knew she could do this. I whispered encouragement to her – but I knew she didn't hear me. She was deep inside of herself.

Then she looked up – and the venom spewed.

"I hated you guys before even coming in here. I was crying in the foyer because I thought, 'You guys didn't kill my brother. And I shouldn't feel this hatred because you didn't even do anything to my brother. But I still have that feeling. And I'm sitting here thinking, do they understand what I'm trying to say or do they care?'"

The air was tense. Her voice and manner were unusually confrontational. Again, I was surprised at this other side of victims telling their stories.

Then she couldn't stop crying – heaving sobs.

I wondered about tissues. I had requested a Kleenex box as part of the preparation. And then I noticed a roll of toilet paper at the end of the table – just out of reach. One of the men listening rolled it over to her.

"We don't have tissues in here," René explained to me.

I nodded – remembering a presentation I had heard in a workshop on grief. According to the presenter, toilet paper was preferable when grieving. The tissue just rolls off – doesn't have to be pulled. Grief needs to flow. The tissue needs to be stronger and rougher than Kleenexes.

She thanked him, and she took an extra-long strip of it and then ripped it off with a flourish.

Then she continued. "There's another lesson that I learned. It doesn't matter what the person is. Everyone has somebody that loves him, and that wants him to be alive and that needs him. So, killing a person is not the answer. Killing doesn't solve anything."

Now she's laughing and crying. She looks around the room.

There are at least six aquariums. "I look at your beautiful fish, and then I think, 'Anybody who could make a place look so nice and so comfortable and homey-like can't be all bad inside.' And I know you guys were probably just as nervous as we were. But I hated you. I didn't even know you guys. I hadn't even seen your faces but I hated you before coming. It's that hate that I'm talking about. It's the most horrible, horrible thing that a person has to go through. And I hope that someday you guys, who have that hate too, realize that hate has to come out. I've got to do something about it."

She leaned back – allowing the second storyteller to take her place.

Laura, who I thought would be more emotional, was much more composed. She was stronger, more articulate than I had expected.

Actually, both were articulate – even more so than in a support group setting. If there is anything I've learned – there is no better storytelling than when victims meet with offenders. The natural cycling of the traumatized mind is actually creating a forceful, wonderful story in preparation for their unseen foe. They are prepared, they have memorized their victim script.

In contrast, the offenders, faced with the barrage of words from a victim, are tongue-tied. It leaves them powerless. The control shifts – as it should.

Then the lifers began their stories.

The first one told us that he was an adopted kid who had killed his friend in Calgary with a construction gun.

The next one told us that he had stabbed his best friend at the school he went to.

Another told us that he had killed his girlfriend. He was quite emotional.

Another told us about his addictions and how he had killed someone in prison who had called him a loser.

They were all emotional. I had never quite seen this before – the flow of tears – or should I say, the river of tears?

The toilet paper was on the side where the women were sitting because they had been telling their stories. When one of the guys started to cry, Lynne took the roll of toilet paper and pushed it across the table to him.

They had finished telling their stories.

We allowed for interaction.

Lynne – still crying – responded. "You're all such good-looking men…and it makes me wonder. How could somebody looking so nice do something so horrible that they have to be in jail for life? What a waste! You know…I look at your eyes – and I have to look at your eyes because that's how I see the emotions and whether you're taking my words seriously – I can see that you are. If not, you're all pretty damn good actors, and I've been fooled again. But it doesn't matter. I see you cry. That has helped me."

The session took two intense hours, and the toilet paper kept making its rounds.

Lynne was on a high as we left the prison grounds.

I could tell that the growl of her own inner black cloud had diminished now that she had actually been in prison and had encountered four killers.

We walked Lynne and Laura to their cars, wished them well – and made sure they were settled down enough to drive.

René and I stood there, watching them drive down the hill.

René was thrilled at the honest display of emotion.

"Anger is anger. They were all angry. I've always told my clients, 'You can never give me a sob story – poor me, poor me. You can't. I don't care what led up to the point where you killed the person. I don't care what led you to cross that line.' These guys did cross the line when they killed someone. Yet she rolled the toilet paper.

"That was the most important gesture that I have ever seen in anything I have tried to do. She felt compassion towards that guy. It showed me that two human beings, both angry as hell – one whose anger erupted to the point of killing another person – can still be compassionate.

"For me, it was the best thing that could happen to my lifers. They had to meet face to face with what they did.

"Oh my god, that is the best thing that can happen to anyone. A victim and offender. If the victims are given the right to see what they want, and have the offender there, and are willing to take whatever they have been told, then that's what matters to me."

Chapter 15
CHAMELEON

I was aware that what I was doing was experimental...especially in the victim community. If I wanted to introduce it with any kind of credibility, I would need to continue to cultivate my relationship with the restorative justice movement.

I had an advantage. I was there when Restorative Justice was birthed – when it was learning – when this movement became an organized force.

Anyone who was anybody in Corrections and Restorative Justice was there that day – at the national conference – Achieving Satisfying Justice: A Symposium on Implementing Restorative Justice models, March 20, 1997.

One inspirational leader at that time was Rev. Pierre Allard, National Director of Chaplaincy in Correctional Service Canada, who had worked for twenty-five years in the system. He was a powerful orator.

He was one of the first illustrious speakers at the event. "During the darkest period of history," he began in his thick French-Canadian accent, "quite often a small number of men and women scattered throughout the world have been able to reverse the course of historical evolutions. This was possible because they hope beyond all hope.... I feel that, as a group of men and women that have been meeting these last few days, we represent the turning point, and we present a new dynamism."

It was an exclusive gathering – by invitation only – a multi-agency gathering of the experts to develop a "proposal to promote the awareness, exploration, and use of restorative justice approaches by the Canadian Criminal Justice System and the public."

It was a heady experience. I drove with the organizers in a white limousine from the airport to a Vancouver hotel.

Something changed in the restorative justice movement during that symposium. It moved from being a philosophy, an experiment, and an ideal to being a Criminal Justice System funded program. I heard one of the purists say, with deep concern, "I wonder what this will do to the movement when there is actual money behind it – will it be corrupted?"

At that point, none of us had any idea what it would do.

I was a novice, and played a minor part on the panel, "Our experience of the current Criminal Justice System." This is where I met Glenn Flett, a lifer and chronic offender, and many other professionals. I presented my *Fifteen Elements,* as I always did. By this time, they rolled off my tongue.

At this historic symposium, something new was happening to me as well – I was noticed.

Except that it wasn't exactly the crowd I wanted to be noticed by. I was loyal to victims – not offenders. And even though this crowd talked about being victim-centered, I knew that the group I belonged to would not feel they belonged here.

I was keenly aware that I represented the victim community, the majority of whom would not attend a Restorative Justice Symposium.

It seemed there were two distinct camps even in the victim community. At a victim consultation I attended in Ottawa, where I met other parents of murdered children, I felt accepted and respected, but just a little excluded. They held me suspect.

The word forgiveness seemed to follow me wherever I went. Where was my loyalty? Was I a con-lover or loyal to the victim community?

I was feeling the same pressure at this symposium.

Even though I was of the forgiving camp – I felt I needed to represent the two camps that were known as either the "revengeful, angry camp" or as the "advocates."

The organizers kept saying that Restorative Justice put the victim agenda and their story first, but it never felt that way.

It felt as if they, the organizers and mediators, were like chameleons with a nonconscious mimicry of the postures, mannerisms, facial expressions, and behaviors of the other.

I could tell that they shifted their loyalties easily. Sometimes it was on the side of the powerful victim, but more often it was on the side of the powerful offender.

Practitioners seemed to be aware of the victim trauma cloud issue and had learned to respect it. They did not realize that the victim who had experienced a proven, serious crime had the right to be given priority. Their years of working with offenders in prison settings had given them an offender bias.

In the encounters I had attended that were facilitated by professional mediators, there was always one point where they would favor the offender. It was often just a nuance, but to myself and other crime victims who are sensitized to the shifts of power, it was always noticeable. And it was always offensive. There simply could be no excuse or rationalization for murder or other serious crimes in our presence.

I instinctively knew that once there was money behind the offenders' restorative justice programs, they would always present themselves as the more powerful. Money is power.

I understood why the victims would say that, even though the traditional justice system is flawed and doesn't honor us, at least we know where we stand. They couldn't trust the restorative justice programs.

But what else was there?

At least there was hope with this organization. If only I could sensitize them to the issues of victims – perhaps with more awareness?

Shortly after the symposium, I received an invitation from Graham Reddoch, Executive Director of the John Howard Society, to speak at their annual meeting. He, too, had been at the symposium in Vancouver and talked about his latest program, Restorative Resolutions, which provided "sentencing options to the courts in cases where the offender was taking responsibility for his or her actions.... This sentencing plan took into account the victim's concerns...."

The topic I was given was: Victim Empowerment to be feared or welcomed?

I could feel the challenge immediately.

Reddoch was, by this time, already a well-known spokesperson for the criminal justice process in Manitoba. If there was anything in the newspaper to do with Stony Mountain or inmates, the media inevitably asked his opinion – which he gave professionally and with unique expertise and insight. He was respected and articulate.

I didn't know it back then, but Reddoch had traveled much the same journey as I had, being introduced to Restorative Justice through the work of Howard Zehr and Dave Worth when he worked with the Mennonite Central Committee in Alberta. When he was hired as the Executor Director of the John Howard Society, it was with the understanding he would be pushing the organization in the direction of Restorative Justice.

Reddoch was a powerful, key player in Manitoba. He was a good man, with a strong offender orientation – which he needed to do his job well. Also, the John Howard Society in Winnipeg was a national leader as a para-corrections organization.

Even though I had apprehensions about going to their annual meeting, once there, I felt we had a great discussion.

A little while later, I felt honored when Reddoch submitted a play entitled *Connections: a victim awareness play*, for me to read. It had been written by one of his staff, a literacy coach, who was encouraging inmates to understand victim empathy at the same time as they learned to read, write, and express their feelings appropriately.

He invited my program staff and me to come and see it performed in Rockwood, a minimum-security federal prison adjacent to Stony Mountain Institution, just outside of Winnipeg.

We went as a group to see the performance. It was as good as a trip out of town – an exotic outing – with the promise of good theater and inmate actors exploring universal themes.

We were a bit surprised at the caliber of the actors who were very much into the parts they played. Although they didn't have any formal training, they were good. We realized that they were acting out their own reality.

Roger, who played the key role in the drama, was riveting as he delivered his lines. "I knew it was all wrong. I was in too deep – deeper than I'd ever wanted to be. It seemed like there was no way out…that I couldn't get out even if I wanted to. For some reason, I felt I had to see things through to the end…as if it had to happen… like it was my destiny or something. I was just like Raskolnikov."

I couldn't believe that we were hearing a reference to Fyodor Dostoevsky, the Russian novelist who wrote *Crime and Punishment*.

Roger continued, "When I was doing that shit, it was as though I was watching me…. It was a movie, and I was just an actor – you know from Shakespeare – 'All the world's a stage, and….' I know one thing – I didn't like the role I was playing. I wanted to yell, 'Hey director – cut!' but that scene just kept on rolling."

Shakespeare! He was quoting Shakespeare. We were so impressed.

Then at the end of the play, the wife of the murdered man, Marlene, goes to meet Roger and says, "You can't imagine the rage I feel, the pain is unbearable…like your heart's been ripped from your chest. It just hurts. It doesn't stop…. I miss him so much."

Roger responds, "I wish there was something I could do."

Marlene says, "There is nothing you can do."

With that, the play ended – Roger obviously shaken by the meeting.

We enjoyed the play. We enjoyed all of it – and could honestly congratulate the entire cast for an amazing performance.

But later, driving home, we had to answer the real question. Could we, as Victims' Voice, endorse this play as being "victim-friendly?" Would we take a group of crime victims into the institution to see it?

Never! They would be livid.

They would feel betrayed immediately. They would see the true colors of the chameleon.

No – it was a play about inmates talking to each other – rationalizing the crime – meeting the victim – and giving scant recognition of empathy. There was no heroism – no dramatic healing that a crime victim would need to see for this drama to be valid.

Besides – the men looked way too good. They were buff and in great physical shape.

The victims might be envious....

We knew this because that same week – coincidently – we had organized an alumni reunion for the members of our survivors support group that had met regularly ten years previously.

They looked like street people as they had hobbled down the stairs to the basement meeting place or like veterans coming back from war – unkempt, overweight, some on crutches. The simple act of surviving the aftermath of trauma had taken its toll on all of us, and it was visible. We just sat down and laughed and laughed at ourselves. We were a mess.

To bring this group to the play and see the prisoners of our institutions looking so fit – so well looked after – would hurt beyond measure. It would be cruel.

There was nothing satisfying about it – any of it.

I tried to tell Reddoch this in gentle terms – that the play was wonderful but slightly flawed. "Keep it for the men inside – or at least be discreet. The victim community would not look kindly on the success of such a play."

He was disappointed and puzzled.

"Then you write a play that suits your purposes," he said.

He actually offered to write a grant proposal for us. Reddoch was a genius writer.

I thought about it for a while and decided to take him up on the challenge. Our working title was *Disconnections*.

With funding from several sources, we hired a playwright, wrote the play and presented it in a Readers Theater format at different venues around the city. It was an amazing forum for discussion. We met many other victims from the audiences who shared our views – expanded them and even confirmed the need to have this connection with offenders.

But the actual writing process I called the battle of the dramas because, much later, both plays were resurrected, combined, and reshaped into a third drama entitled *Re-connections* that toured Saskatchewan.

That was how Graham Reddoch and I started working together. He could write a genius proposal for any dream I expressed.

For his next venture, on April 15, 1998, Graham held a Consultation Restorative Justice Pilot Project asking the question, "What do victims need?" It was a John Howard Society Mini-Conference in Winnipeg.

I liked going to anything Graham organized – it was always classy, well-attended, and informative.

I had been asked to present my *Fifteen Elements*. I didn't really look in detail at the draft proposal the event was based on but, knowing something of the John Howard program, I assumed that it was created with an offender agenda in mind – so I never spoke to the issues that I was concerned about directly.

I assumed that my job was to simply present the realities of a crime victim – which I did in my description of the fifteen elements. I thought they would speak for themselves.

By this time my *Fifteen Elements* presentation was accepted as a credible contribution to the "victim sensitivity" emphasis that was now part of Corrections Canada, so I was asked to present at various training and professional development sessions. I found myself at a Vancouver Solicitor General Roundtable. Then I was invited to another Roundtable hosted by the Policy Centre for Victim Issues – an important consultation on Victim Issues. I was invited to a Royal Canadian Mounted Police Symposium and then to the National Forum Standing Committee on Justice and Human Rights, followed by a Federal Symposium on National Victims of Crime Awareness Week. It was quite heady.

But I wasn't always in my best form. I remember one particular presentation that I did for the Correctional Management Learning Centre, a national Victim Liaison Coordinator Training.

I had flown into Ottawa late the night before and was presenting first thing in the morning. I knew this was an extremely important presentation – mainly because I had become close friends with one of the organizers and knew that she had a lot riding on my performance.

By this time, I could have recited the stories in my sleep. However, suffering from jet lag, I went into my presentation on auto pilot – and plunged into the element of identity devastation where I describe the plight of victims finding themselves no longer acceptable. Communities operate like a living organism, and need to have a harmony within themselves to survive. Consequently, they will marginalize any threat to their unity.

At least that's what I wanted to say – but in my sleepy stupor I substituted "orgasm" for "organism." I actually said, "Communities operate like a living, vibrant orgasm." I looked over my audience, all smartly-dressed, professional federal employees – and they were sitting there stoic faced – watching me. Not a facial muscle had moved. It felt surreal.

I just burst out laughing. "Did you hear what I said? I am so sorry." And then, to my horror, I couldn't get it straight. I kept mixing it all up. It was a gong show.

By this time, they were laughing – I was laughing – and the rest of the presentation somehow mysteriously had a heightened erotica that I couldn't shake. Everything I said became suggestive and provocative.

I was mortified.

It didn't help that someone said it had been the highlight of their training. I thought I would never be allowed outside the MCC office again.

In any case, after one of these presentations, I was invited to meet with members of the Restorative Justice Unit in Ottawa before I flew home. They wanted to talk to me.

I remember sitting on the office couch, two of the organizers of the Restorative Justice Unit opposite me. They started talking about their excitement that I was lending my name to this new program in Winnipeg.

"What?"

"Yes – the proposal by Graham Reddoch. You will work so well with him. Your name assures us that it is victim-centered."

"What? Victim-centered?"

"This – it's all here."

And they then handed me the proposal. I skimmed it quickly. Yes, it was very similar to what I had heard talked about at the Consultation, but this time my name had been added to it as someone who had attended and, thereby, was endorsing it. I was under the names of people that were listed as endorsers.

I was horrified. The program was offender-centered – as it should be. It's important to work with offenders, but to promote an offender rehabilitation program as victim-centered would be false advertising. It might deceive a defenseless victim into thinking it was for them – exclusively. The system would be revictimizing them all over again.

I could feel my hair stand on end. The tumultuous clouds were gathering. This wasn't only about me – I had to defend the entire victim community.

"I don't endorse it as it stands," I told them. "This is a misunderstanding. I only attended the consultation because I thought my workshop of *Fifteen Elements* would be the fifteen reasons why this proposal does not address the victims' needs. I have no intention of being involved – as a victim advocate. It's a great program for offenders…. In fact, I promise you that I will be critical of it – in terms of victim sensitivity – to anyone who asks."

To myself, I didn't think it would matter much what I thought….

But by the time I came home to Winnipeg, I heard via the grapevine that the Ottawa RJ Unit had actually rejected the proposal.

I was horrified – realizing that the John Howard Society had lost a great deal of money because of my reaction. They said it was because of some other reasons, but I secretly felt responsible.

I couldn't imagine their disappointment.

I expected to never hear from Graham again.

So, when he asked me to lunch a little while later, I was reluctant to accept. I expected that I would receive a tongue-lashing like no other. After all, he was a gifted orator.

I think I tried to get out of it – but he was insistent, so I agreed.

I owed him an explanation, at least.

We met at a Salisbury House on St. Mary's Road.

I just ordered a cup of coffee, expecting it to be a quick meeting, but he waved my initial apologies aside. Then he said that he had a new proposal – and asked if I would look at it for approval.

He shoved the paper across the table towards me.

I looked at it – shocked. By this time, I was paranoid. It seemed I was being pressured from all sides, from all different kinds of restorative justice initiatives – to endorse, promote, or enhance.

I shook my head. "No, I'm not going to look at it…. I will take your word for it that it's great for offenders, but I won't touch it."

"Just skim it – I think you will like it."

I shrank back. "I'm not touching it. You can do whatever you like, Graham. I won't criticize what you do…. You've done excellent work with offenders, but I won't have my name next to yours. Go around for other endorsers – the city is full of them."

"Just look at it."

"I can't." I would not betray the others – the other invisible victims that were sitting at the table – I just couldn't.

We parted politely but abruptly. I thought he would never speak to me again.

But he wouldn't stop.

Graham had the patience of Job. He set up another meeting. "Just tell me what you would envision," he insisted.

Then he interviewed me. He prodded me.

I was beginning to realize that what was obvious to me – wasn't as obvious to the other practitioners.

And then he came up with another genius proposal.

He put my program in the middle of the encounter experience, with Mediation Services and the John Howard Society playing supportive roles.

This was the dream!

The following abstract was written in 2003.

Three community agencies, Victims' Voice, John Howard Society, and Mediation Services, all with extensive involvement in addressing criminal justice concerns, are proposing a unique partnership that will enable victims to design and control their individual role in the justice-making process. It will allow victims to safely contact those who have harmed them through the development and negotiation of a contract. This approach is intended to address their needs, their concerns and their hopes in a way that is respectful of both the contract holders and the offender. Victims often express anxiety over unmet needs and concerns about the offender and the offense, especially regarding information that is not otherwise provided by the court process. Through Contracting Safe Justice, it is our expectation that safe, supportive, and respectful opportunities will be provided for victims and offenders to find justice and peace.

After the proposal was accepted, I dared to set up two programs.

One was called Victim Companions, a program designed to accompany crime victims on their journey no matter where they were, who they were, and what their goals. It was built on the premise that healing would come by simply supporting a crime victim with whatever they needed – basic support. Their needs were fairly obvious – information, validation, and a safe place to process their changing world.

The second program was called Safe Justice Encounters. It was set up to partner with the John Howard Society and Mediation Services. I felt that we had developed the perfect victim-focused, victim-driven, and victim-initiated restorative justice program.

It was a program where victims were in control of the entire encounter process. They were front and center. They could outline their needs, their expectations, and then we would take their custom-made plan and set up a meeting with the offender.

We were in the final stages of editing the draft proposal for a substantial amount of money that had, in essence, already been accepted.

We had been invited to design an encounter that perfectly met all the criteria. It was going to be our prototype.

We were so excited.

Chapter 16
HOUSE

Then I received a cryptic message from René Durocher.

"We need to have breakfast."

He was already sitting in the back of the restaurant when I arrived – in exactly the place I would have chosen.

I slid into the booth opposite him.

The waitress hovered. We both ordered – something simple – coffee and two pieces of toast. He ordered rye bread.

I shoved the cutlery aside and laid down my notebook.

He looked unusually stressed. He looked drawn – reluctant.

"I can't do this," he said.

I was aghast! I knew he was talking about our dream program, apparently wanting to withdraw.

I tried not to panic.

"What can't you do?" I asked softly.

"I can't meet with him – the offender."

I was stunned.

"Has the institution objected to us doing this?"

He shook his head. "No, nothing like that. I can't meet with the offender because he is a sexual offender."

I nodded. "Yes – we know that. We've always known that."

"Wilma, he's a sexual offender," he repeated the words, emphasizing every word…as if something had changed.

I was perplexed. "We've always known that – he assaulted his sister…. That's why we are doing this…."

He leaned back. "I can't work with a sexual offender," he said flatly – unmovable.

I studied him. "Is this personal?"

"Yes…. When I was on the inside, we never had anything to do with sexual offenders – except to shank them when we walked by them."

I was stunned. I would never have seen this coming.

This was our first breakthrough in working with encounters. This was a huge opportunity in our program of Safe Justice Encounters. This was big. When I had proposed the program, I had no idea if we would attract even one victim or what it would look like.

No sooner had we begun advertising this program to select a target victim market, when we had a response from someone who looked as if they were the perfect candidate.

The woman was in her thirties and had been sexually assaulted by her older brother when she was a teen. After serving his time, he was now in a minimum-security institution waiting for his parole. She wanted to visit with him before he was released, to test what their outside relationship might be.

Pat was a professional – articulate – and precise with her expectations. I had met with her a few times and briefed her about our program. After I had approved her, I had sent word to René to meet with the offender, and gain his cooperation. Together with the skills of a professional facilitator, we would then set up an encounter.

It was simple – at least this part was.

But now René was sitting opposite me – telling me that he wouldn't even do an initial meeting because the man's file classified him as a sexual offender. Apparently, René didn't associate with sex offenders.

I just stared at him, trying to get my mind around this. It was disgusting. Criminals were criminals. They were all the same. What difference was there between stealing a million dollars or assaulting someone? Both were violations of the law of the land and of decency.

"Really, René?" I laid into him. "Do you really think he is any different than any other criminal in prison?"

And I'm not sure about all that I said. I was furious. He had promised! He owed me one – he owed everyone in Canada this one.

He sat there looking utterly miserable.

"Wilma, I can't…." He pleaded for understanding. "I just can't…."

"What's wrong with a sex offender? He hasn't taken a life – he has a sexual desire that went wrong and chose to act it out inappropriately. It's a violation. It is criminal, but no one was killed. How can you have more sympathy for a killer than a sexual predator?"

I was blunt.

"Sexual offenders are worse," he said.

"Really, René – more serious than a killer?"

He nodded.

I couldn't believe him. "Why, René? Help me understand this," I asked.

I could tell that he was as miserable as I was. He opened up his mouth a few times to answer me – but there were no words. I waited, sipping my coffee – looking out the window, trying to deal with my own disappointment. I had not seen this one coming in a million years. I had thought the stigmatization of victims would be the problem. I thought no one might come forward. Not this.

Finally, he cleared his throat. I had never seen him so shaken.

"I think I know why," he said softly.

He looked tired, deflated, and hollow. "I was sexually assaulted when I was a kid…. That's why I hate sex offenders."

"You never told me that!"

"I know – I never thought of myself as a victim like that. I don't think I've remembered that for years – and years – ever since I left home."

He was shaking his head in disbelief. "But I think that is what it has been…."

He looked terrible.

I felt terrible for putting him into this position of remembering. The stupid program was all but forgotten....

"I'm so sorry...so sorry! Who was it?" I asked gently.

He shrugged – his face so pale.

I leaned forward. "Why don't you just tell me when it happened? It might help."

He took a deep breath.

"After my father's bloody assault, my mother went to work. Nothing worked out, and I was put into foster care. That's when I started to attend church.

"Every kid at six or seven years old was formally introduced into the church by baptism, communion, and confirmation. As an altar boy, you can serve communion in the church. There was mass every morning – and I was always ready to serve.

"I loved to go to church. I can still remember my First Communion when the priest said that I would either be a brilliant statesman or a great criminal."

I remembered the school gymnasium.... He had used that memory over and over again. Having heard his stories many times, I was surprised at his accuracy, his recall.

He continued. "I liked the mass. It was a ritual that I could count on. It felt comfortable.

"At that time, the priests were very involved in the day-to-day activity of their parishioners. They would visit every family – often controlling them. I was taught to believe that the priest was a voice from God and someone who could not do anything wrong. I truly believed that they were the best people in the world because that is the way they were introduced to me.

"And that is where the nightmare happened in my life.

"I have never spoken about this before – not to anybody. The first time I was sexually assaulted was when I was seven. It was by the priest after I had made my First Communion.

"We were in the back, preparing for mass – when he pulled me aside and touched me. Then he made me touch him, then he took me in his mouth.

"When you are a kid – only seven years old – you don't even know what this means. You don't have a clue, you just freeze, and you cannot talk to no one because it is the priest.

"Very carefully, he aroused me – sexualized me – and played me.

"I saw him every day, so he had his way with me every day – and I could not tell the family I lived with.

"That priest did that for about six to eight months, almost daily. After a while, I was living it. There is nothing you can say, you just scream and cry.

"I am sure that he did this to all the other kids, but we never talked. We were taught to be very secretive, don't say a word, and it is okay. It is religion. They can brainwash you with anything because they are used to preaching, and all that stuff. Then they can take you for the ride of your life, and you don't even know you are taking the ride of your life.

"The second sexual assault happened when I was living at home. I was about twelve at this time. My mother had managed to get her life together, collected all her children, and we were living at home.

"My mother had a friend. I don't know his first name. I cannot remember ever calling him by his first name. I found out later that he had been a priest in the Catholic Church and had been defrocked. He traveled all over Quebec selling hair growth products – something that was popular in the mid-fifties.

"At one point, he asked my mother, 'Would you mind if I take one of your sons with me for two or three days?'

"This would be a huge saving for my mother – to have one less mouth to feed for a few days.

"I went with him to remote places on one of these trips – 400 or 500 miles away from home. It was winter – terrible conditions. The snowbanks were twenty feet high on both sides of the road. When we got to the first house and rang the bell, the man let us in. He knew the priest because he had bought products from him before. And we sometimes would stay the night. I think there were two bedrooms, but we ended up in the same bedroom. I was naive. I guess I hadn't learned yet. That was when I was sexually assaulted the second time.

"It was brutal. He assaulted me like a son of a bitch. He started by taking me in his mouth, and then he tried to get his penis inside me. It didn't work. I was mad. I was crying but I couldn't run away. It was the middle of winter and I only had an old jacket. I didn't own many clothes back then. We were in the middle of nowhere. Even if I had run, I would probably have died from exposure in an hour or two.

"When I got back to the city after the trip, I didn't even go into the house. I ran away. I didn't want to be questioned. I didn't want to be asked for anything. I was afraid.

"I was angry with my mother because she was the one who was instrumental in pushing me into the relationship with the priest.

"Actually, I don't think my mother knew about the sexual assaults. I never talked to her about it. But I blamed her."

He paused and just sat there – looking exhausted.

By this time our trauma clouds had become one – and I could feel it stalking both of us. It was winning, and we were helpless.

"I'm so sorry!" I said over and over again.

He looked up. His eyes were dark – glistening.

He continued. "Imagine. I was a child – only seven – when this happened the first time. I didn't know why I was fighting against the world. Oh my god! The long-term ravages of sexual predators.

"I hate religion and the Catholic Church with a passion. I never went back to any religion after that. I do believe in God, but I don't believe that God needs a middleman to deal with me. If he does need a middleman, these kinds of priests aren't it. I turned my back on the church.

"When a father figure comes and violates you in this way, and inside you are feeling it is all wrong, yet the attention feels good, it gets all mixed up.

"And it comes out in aggression against everyone.

"And then you blame your mother for the assault.

"There was nothing left for me. Nothing to hold onto.

"As far as I was concerned, I had no father and no mother.

"I had to fend for myself."

The waitress removed everything from the table and slipped us the bill.

We hadn't eaten anything....

We just sat there – stunned.

"You don't have to do this, René. We'll find someone else. There are others who can do this. I wouldn't want you to have to 'look after' this man. I completely understand now.... I'm so sorry I pushed you so hard."

He paused.

And it was as if he was finally seeing me.

"No – I need to do this. I can do this."

And he did.

It turned out to be one of those encounters that met every one of our expectations. Pat was able to lay out her plan carefully, concisely and descriptively. Her brother was at times disgusting, even though he felt his issues. I could tell it was hard. He was still trying to control her. I was glad for René who was at his side – a stabilizing force.

And then they came to an agreement. It was surprising. Just when we thought they would never be able to agree on anything, together they came up with an agreement. They would occasionally meet in a mall, to have coffee as brother and sister. But she would never bring her children. They might eventually have family gatherings, but these gatherings would always be supervised.

When Pat expressed a desire to see him once he was on parole, he seemed taken aback. He agreed to all of her restrictions and seemed delighted that she offered even just a suggestion of further support.

And then we left.

It was perfect! We thought we could have left it at that.

But the agreed process of these encounters was to show her the video of the entire conversation.

When we viewed it together, Pat just fell apart and cried and cried and cried.

We were a little shocked until she explained. Now that she was viewing the video in a safe room without the offender's presence, she could see him through an entirely different lens. He had aged. He had suffered. She felt for him.

According to her, the encounter had been the negotiation, and the video debrief had been the healing.

I was shocked that it had been the video.

She was so appreciative of our efforts.

After she had left the room, René smiled.

"It was worth it," he said.

We both knew that there had been two encounters that day. He, too, had met his nemesis cloud and negotiated a new peace. He had forgiven.

For me, this meant that the program was working.

We continued the program.

The most memorable encounter had been between a mother and the man who had murdered her daughter.

We had been forced to strip it right down to the bone. Our usual mediators were unavailable. So, it was just the three of us – Graham, acting as a fill-in mediator, René as the contact, the support person for the offender, and I. We had driven with the victim's mother to a northern CSC facility where the meeting was being held.

I had prepped the mother. René had prepped the lifer, and Graham chaired the encounter.

It was so perfect!

The magical moment in each of the dialogues we organized was when we asked both parties how they would like to be treated if they met each other by chance in a shopping mall. Did they want to be greeted? Did they want to walk past each other without any sign of recognition? Did they want the other person to move quickly out of view, or was it okay to continue to do whatever they had planned?

The answers were always fascinating. One woman had said, "If I'm with my children, I want you to leave immediately on sight. If I'm alone – we could even say 'hi,' but that is all." Another said, "If we are in a public place, we can just pretend we don't know each other. If I'm walking down a street and there is no one around – could you walk in the other direction and disappear as quickly as possible."

In this case, the mother and the murderer were able to work out a rather complicated, new relationship. The hurt was still there, but some of the fears had been assuaged.

We had built a safe bridge between the two worlds. Not everyone might want to cross over to the other side – but those who did needed a safe bridge.

And then it crashed. It was shortly after the "perfect encounter" that the funders paid us a visit and told us that the pilot program we had spent two years developing was being shut down. After an informal survey conducted by the funders, we heard that the reviews of our Safe Justice Encounters program were inconclusive. Not every encounter had been successful.

More importantly, they, the Correctional Service Canada Restorative Justice Unit, had decided that our program was not restorative justice. Apparently, it was more a victim services program. Therefore, all funding was terminated.

I could not believe what I was hearing.

From the very beginning, the authors and program directors of Restorative Justice had always assured me their goal of restorative justice was to provide an equal platform for both victim and offender – but it needed to be victim focused.

And here I had delivered exactly what everyone had been asking for – a program that assured a platform for victims that now matched the platform of the offenders – yet assured the victims of being treated with deference. I had thought Restorative Justice was all about equal opportunity of victim and offender – trying to be perfectly balanced. Yet it couldn't be.

Because of the inherent imbalance of power between the two, the victim's needs – which should be paramount – were often overlooked.

I thought our program would complete the restorative justice experience – and fashion a valid victim restorative justice alternative.

They admitted that if an encounter was offender-initiated and offender-directed, it was Restorative Justice and within the mandate of Correctional Service Canada. However, if it was victim-initiated and victim-oriented, it was Victim Services and not within their mandate.

This had been my fear from the very beginning. My victim friends had been right – it was an offender-driven program. René got the gymnasium; I got the classroom. Offenders had all kinds of non-profit, para-corrections organizations – charities that helped with rehabilitation programs; victims had only customer service desks in various offender-driven organizations.

No one had any idea of how one-sided the world of justice appeared to victims.

I was stunned.

After the funders had left, we cleaned up the coffee cups as we processed.

Graham wasn't as discouraged as I was. He continued his questions. "What would it take?" he kept asking everyone – including me.

"Another leg," I said offhandedly. I had in the past often used the metaphor of a three-legged stool. I maintained that until the stool had three balanced legs, justice couldn't happen. We had the offender's leg. We were in the process of developing a restorative justice leg that carried so much promise. What we were lacking was a victim program for the third leg. The third leg was missing and, until there was a stand-alone program for victims, the stool would always tip.

This time Graham didn't let it lie.

"What would it take to build that leg for victims?" he asked. "Did we learn anything in the successful Victim Companions program that we could expand?"

He was persistent.

I nodded. I could have continued the Victim Companions program because it had proven itself. But – it was in the wrong place. It was a pilot project being housed in the MCC national offices. It was a cubicle – a space enclosed by dividers – with no promise of confidentiality that victims need.

It was just another desk housed in a larger organization with different priorities.

We needed more.

We all need someplace we can call home. We, as a group of parents of murdered children, had felt like nomads. Even the simple need to have a consistent meeting place was difficult. We were evicted from one dark, dingy church basement to another. We needed a place to meet for coffee. I can't count the number of times I had made an appointment to meet a crime victim in some north-end café and no one would show. Not that they were irresponsible – they were the ones who had wanted to meet with me. Later, I would find out that they hadn't been able to make it because something had happened. There was always some form of trauma. Lifestyle disorganization. Transitions. Depression.

I understood. After a murder one has to change everything! Place, job, values. Victims are nomads in their own lives.

We needed a kind of sanctuary – a safe place of our own.

In my mind's eye, I saw the offender in the big house – the prison. I saw the entire Criminal Justice System in the courthouse. I saw the police at their station. I saw the ex-convicts in their halfway houses. Everyone has a house. Even Ronald McDonald has a house. Why couldn't we just have a house?

Almost in tears, I whispered. "They just need a house of their own."

I felt like a little child – I just needed to go back to my room with my blankie. We didn't even have a safe room – much less a house.

"What kind of house?"

"A safe house that would feel like home with stand-alone programs. It needs to have independent funding, be separate from the Criminal Justice System to keep it loyal to victims," I said. "It needs to have a kitchen, coffee…."

Then Floyd Wiebe walked into the room.

I had met Floyd at the Northern Lights Conference, a Compassionate Friends International Conference, where I had presented two workshops on my *Fifteen Elements*. Filled with his own grief, in desperation, he had driven to Brandon, Manitoba, to hear me speak. He had just lost his twenty-year-old son, TJ, to a senseless murder in Winnipeg.

After that, he had become a tireless advocate for victim rights. We always had an understanding that, even though we came at things differently, we shared an ultimate goal – to help others.

Since he had not heard our kitchen conversation, I repeated the question, "Floyd, what do victims need?"

I tried to open up his imagination even more. "If you won a billion dollars in a 649 draw, what would you do? In other words, if money wasn't a problem, what would your wildest dream be?"

"I'd build them a house," he said simply.

We were all astonished.

Then he added another critical insight.

"A house near the courthouse."

His experience was different than mine.

The trial concerning the murder of his son had lasted five and a half months. He had experienced the wear and tear of the justice process.

Then we laughed. Both of us could see it, feel it. It would be perfect. What a relief to even say it!

Graham was both listening and watching.

After Floyd left, I told Graham that my interest in Restorative Justice was over. I was no longer going to work at anything to do with programming for dialogues and Restorative Justice.

If I did continue in this field, I would keep the two fields distinct and separate – continuing either with victim awareness or with offender issues – but not the two together.

It was over – it was good-bye!

But I couldn't just walk out the door this time. I had to close the program down. Farewells were not easy to do…. The mourning was intense.

Chapter 17
ARREST

I didn't know it but a new set of dark, writhing, reptilian clouds were about to pounce – very similar to that first night when they were waiting for us on our bed.

It was November 30, 2006 – the anniversary of Candace's disappearance. Twenty-two years after her murder – the police called us.

I'll never forget that day. I opened up the door. Three uniformed men were standing there – tall – all dressed in black.

They introduced themselves to us.

Al Bradbury, whom we already knew from prior visits, made a point of making sure we knew that Sergeant Shipley was the man in charge. They made themselves comfortable in our tiny living room. There were five of us – all dressed in black – sitting in my predominantly white living room.

Bradbury leaning forward.

"We found him," he said.

My mind was racing. After years of dealing with the public suspicion of Cliff, I wondered if this would be a ploy. I wondered if we said, "Who?" they would say, "You!" And then I would grab Cliff's hand and pull him into the kitchen to call a lawyer. They were not going to take my husband. They were not going to scapegoat him.

Bradbury, completely unaware of my thoughts, waited then said it again, "We found him."

I nodded and waited. They waited.

"We know who did it," he said, watching us.

I still nodded. I still couldn't say anything. From the corner of my eye, I knew Cliff was having as much trouble as I was – wondering what their next words would be. Our minds were racing in a million directions.

They were waiting for a response.

"Are you sure?" I said, finally.

"Yes."

I looked at each one of them separately. They all nodded. It was easy to tell that they were all united.

I still didn't know how to move the conversation along, to hide our own fears, and still release them to tell us more.

Finally, I thought of the perfect question. "Do we know him?"

"No, you don't," they said.

"Are you sure we don't know him?" we asked, feeling the first wave of relief.

"Yes – we are sure. You don't know him."

"Are you sure?"

Bradbury leaned slightly forward. "And I just want to let you know...it isn't anyone known to your family."

They must have said it a dozen times in different ways before I was convinced this wasn't some kind of trick.

"Aren't you relieved?"

We nodded. Our poor, traumatized minds could not absorb it. It was hard to erase twenty-two years of careful, solid defenses in one second.

As we sat, still stunned, they began a long description of what the process had been, how they had acquired funding, started to isolate the DNA, and had finally made a match in December....

"What are the next steps? Is there a plan?" we asked.

They told us that they would be picking him up in two to six weeks and that they had a team of twelve officers working on it. It was pending.

And slowly, very slowly, I began to realize the magnitude of their visit. There really was a person out there with a name who was soon going to be charged with the first-degree murder of our daughter. In time we would find out his name. We were no longer going to be part of an unsolved mystery.

We again talked about the next steps. Who could we tell? No one.

Could we tell our adult children? We had two children, both married. Odia and her husband, Larry Reimer, lived in Altona, one hour south of us. Syras had married Natasha Fay six months before, and they lived close by in an apartment near Pembina Highway. Could we at least tell them?

Yes, they said. Then, putting on their heavy leather jackets, their shiny black shoes, they shook our hands and left.

"Keep warm," I said, as they walked out into the cold, winter air. It was the only way I could express my appreciation at that moment. It was so inadequate. Many times since, I wished I could replay that visit to let them know how much we appreciated their work and their care of us, but right then, it was as if we were living in a bubble lost in time, dealing with a thousand leftover issues.

I closed the door.

It was over. They had found him!

When we told our adult children that the police had found the person responsible for the murder of Candace, Odia's first response was, "We don't need this. I don't even want it."

We could feel the clouds closing in.

I could see the fear….

This dread of the justice system came from the many stories that we had read and heard about other crime victims who had encountered the Criminal Justice System. So often, I had seen normal grief and murder trauma turn into something quite different after a trial. It seemed as if it would suck optimistic victims into its systems, trapping them in endless processes and then spewing them out at the end – like dried, dead bones – their spirit unrecognizable.

On May 6, 2007, six months later, the accused was charged with first-degree murder.

To announce the arrest, the Chief of Police wanted us to join them for the press conference. When we got to the Public Safety Building, we were ushered into the press room. Winnipeg Police Chief Jack Ewatski read the Media Release.

They had entitled it *Project Angel Leads to Arrest in 1984 Candace Derksen Homicide.* The statement covered the entire story.

The press statement ended with....

At this time, new leads were established and pursued.

As a result of a comprehensive investigation known as "Project Angel," the Winnipeg Police Service has identified a suspect in the murder of Candace Derksen.

This morning the Cold Case Unit arrested the suspect. A 43-year-old man of Winnipeg, has been charged with First Degree Murder and is now in police custody.

Once the police chief had completed his statement, Cliff read our statement. "We are grateful for this moment. Of course, with this comes a renewed sense of sadness that has never left, and never will, at the loss of our daughter. It also reminds us of the horrors of her passing."

He added, "We had actually given up hope. We were already prepared to live with this mystery. This just leaves us stunned and reeling with many emotions." And then he thanked the Chief, the police, the investigators, and our amazing Winnipeg community again.

After the press conference, some of the reporters followed us to our home for more in-depth interviews. I invited them in. These were our storytellers.

I was also hearing through the grapevine that I wasn't doing very well. Sometimes I was down – but sometimes I was up. I wanted to live with integrity, and I wanted the stories swirling around me to have integrity – if they were going to swirl – and apparently, they were – I was going to have a say.

I started blogging, beginning each blog with the question: Would you meet with him? In some ways, I was playing with the whole concept of forgiveness that was still appearing as our one and only theme.

That same night, unexpectedly, the doorbell rang around ten o'clock.

Standing at the door was a couple that we had come to know. He was involved with police work; her mother had been murdered. They were the perfect experts for the moment.

I had come to know her after her mother's murder. At the time, I had been impressed with her inner strength and, especially, her ability to articulate the issues she was facing. She was beautiful, a gifted public speaker and could mobilize the people around her.

But I had gotten a call from her in the middle of the preliminary hearing – and she had been incoherent, completely undone. I couldn't believe how this confident, young woman with so much inner resolve could be so shredded by a process that was intended to bring justice to her family. I just ached for her – and listened to her the very best I could. But I took notes. She did too. Since they had recently been through a trial, they had come to tell us what to expect.

We invited them in.

For Cliff and I, the entire day felt like *déjà vu*. We felt we had lived this before. It seemed like a familiar plot. An odd rerun of the first beginnings when Candace had been found murdered.

There is something called a circular narrative plot found in all the classic works of literature, from oral anecdotes to modern cinema. We saw the same circular format emerging in our story, similar themes playing themselves out.

There was now this ten o'clock visit – reminiscent of the day Candace's body was found. It had been at the end of that day, around ten o'clock, when the man appeared at our door. His visit had forced us to be very intentional about how we would deal with the aftermath of murder.

There was the same touching column in the paper. One written twenty-three years ago by Lesley Hughes, now one by Lindor Reynolds, expressing the same sentiment. "What we can't do is reclaim our sense of innocence and our belief that children are precious, not just to us but to everyone else."

There was the theme of friends, who had remained friends for twenty-three years, a bond even stronger than before, who all touched base with us. Some sent cards, some resorted to the new social media that was emerging, and some called.

And as before, the newspaper headlines picked up on the forgiveness theme just as they had so long ago.

It felt like a rerun.

Our children – now adults – grilled our visitors. First of all, they wanted to know about the court process in detail. The couple were able to outline the process, the bail hearing, the preliminary hearing, and eventually the trial that included a Judge, Crown and Defense.

Our children wanted to know the social and emotional impact.

The woman talked about the social aspect, the need to have people around. She described how, after the preliminary hearing, she had floundered and decided that for her to survive the trial, she would need people. She organized her friends and family and coped much better because of it.

They talked about the spiritual aspect of a trial. To us, it was obvious that they had been very intentional throughout the entire process – exactly what we wanted to be.

When the couple left, we processed it all again as a family and talked at length about how to prepare in all of these areas: physically, socially, spiritually, and mentally.

Then we all headed for our beds. I wondered about the dark presence. Would it make an appearance? Now that we had a name – even if it wasn't proven – it was a new reality.

Would the reptilian cloud come snarling with a new vehemence? Would it be on our bed again? Would it come into our lives again? It did come – later.

Chapter 18
REDEMPTION

Meanwhile, Graham, René and I couldn't forget how close we had come to creating that "perfect encounter" before the crash of our Safe Justice program.

We analyzed, dreamt and pondered it all incessantly.

Graham particularly could not let go of the "house" idea that Floyd and I had mentioned. He wrote the first proposal, called The Samaritan's Inn: Creating A Safe Hospitality Home for Victims of Crime, then started looking for a house.

He actually found the perfect house. It had been law offices. The lawyer, whose lawyer son had passed away, had listed the house for sale, with no offers. We even received permission from MCC Canada to see if they would be interested in buying it. Graham had even approached the realtor to see if we could negotiate a charitable donation receipt along with a much smaller purchase price. But at that point someone else made an offer, and the house was gone.

Then things changed for both René and Graham. They were no longer connected with the John Howard Society – and yet wanted to continue their work within the justice process. René had an opportunity to hold a Life Line contract and Graham wanted to work in an organization that stressed rehabilitation. So, they decided to start a St. Leonard's organization.

The St. Leonard's Society wasn't known in Winnipeg and had been founded to give people who have been in trouble with the law a place to live and an opportunity to remove the stigma of being a former prisoner through guidance, counseling, and understanding. They excelled in rehabilitation.

I needed to shift focus as well. Consequently, after deciding to drop the dream of successful victim-offender encounters as part of my program, I resumed a healing emphasis with a new word – Resilience. I would focus only on the inner healing.

Even though we were now working in two distinct communities, the victim community and the offender community, we still had a common goal.

And a common cloud problem.

There was my work with victims, where I would have to drop my guard and love them where they were at. It wasn't always easy because their clouds were dark, fuming and full of red-hot cannon balls ready to be catapulted in every direction. Often, I was the target. For me – to remain vulnerable was my only defense.

Then there were the co-dependent, violent, often snarky and cynical offender clouds, rattling chains. Crazymakers. With these I found that I was constantly needing to fight blindly through my own crazymaking clouds and remain forgiving.

I relied on Graham's clarity. Once again in his genius-proposal-writing mode, he designed Journey for Justice that would oversee the journeys of offenders and victims, which were presented as separate programs but would need to be overseen by the same board with representation from both.

It was the ideal – our chosen goal. It had two houses, one for the offenders and one for the victims – the perfect satisfying justice paradigm.

To be perfectly balanced, they invited me to the table, as a parent of a murdered child, and another couple, parents of a murderer, a son who had killed his best friend.

Ordinarily, there would have been no problem with the two parent groups getting along perfectly – but, given the circumstances, right from the onset, it was like trying to mix water and oil. The black cloud was there right between us – unseen by the others – but repelling us from each other.

The couple started missing meetings. If they were present, I withdrew – feeling genuinely ill. Both groups were unhappy and the board chair at the time sensed all of this.

It came to a head at one meeting.

I'll always remember the scene. It was in the MCC boardroom – a place of such calmness and peace. There we were. I was sitting at the end of the table near the kitchen, making sure everyone had access to the coffee and goodies. At the head of the table was the president of the organization of this pilot project.

His name was Alan Libman. I didn't know much about him, except that he was a defense lawyer and a close friend of René's.

Libman, who had been practicing law with Legal Aid Manitoba for fifteen years, was at that time well known for his work with James Lockyer, who had founded the organization, Association in Defense of the Wrongly Convicted (AIDWC) in Canada.

For me – he was a lawyer. Every good board has one lawyer because of their skill in building a good argument and then deconstructing it at will. I had seen it done many times, and I was frankly awed by this skill. They were like magicians with the truth – making it appear and disappear at will. I had also learned that this game with truth had its place in the discerning justice process. We had to see everything from every possible angle.

And there he was – sitting at the head of the table.

Then early in the meeting, in front of the board members, Libman started blaming me for the reluctance of the offender's parents, insinuating that I was keeping them from the table. I don't think it was that strong an accusation – he was always polite, but I felt the accusation – or at least the probing questions.

In any case, I saw red. And I saw all kinds of dark clouds.

I took a moment to regroup. How could I explain this invisible force, this black cloud, that they were all blind to? What example could I give them to illustrate a historic, dramatic, irreconcilable conflict? The Middle East came to mind.

"Don't you understand?" I began. "Yes – you are looking at two groups of people that have been victimized by the crime – the offender's family and the victim's family. You would think they would understand each other and would have compassion for each other. But look at Israel and Palestine. You can't imagine two peoples that have been more victimized – yet they will never see eye to eye because they are competing for the same land. Because of their victimization, both have lost their land and both are looking for a place to call home – to be safe.

"There hasn't been a peace plan that has been able to work!

"Understandably! How do you expect victim and offender families to work together? Just as with the Middle East, they are from two different countries – blaming, fighting and competing for attention. They are both fragmented. They can't help each other! You can't ever put them in the same room and expect them to be objective and generous. They are two desperate peoples – just trying to survive. And if you can't see that, I can't help you anymore!"

And I was ready to leave the table.

But something happened. I could almost visibly see Libman have an "aha" moment. His eyes changed; his posture changed.

"I can see that now," he said simply.

I wondered what brilliant thing I had said to win an argument with a defense lawyer – and that's when I remembered that he was Jewish!

I was a bit horrified – and relieved – all at the same time.

After that we worked through a lot of things at that board table but I never had to explain any of the victim issues again. He had seen the dark, black clouds – probably better than the rest of us.

Meanwhile, St. Leonard's programs were growing. René had been hired as the Volunteer Coordinator.

171

Graham worked his magic and wrote yet another proposal, the Paying Forward Project, which was approved by Correctional Service Canada with cooperation between MCC Canada and St. Leonard's Society. It was based on organized dialogues with surrogate community members and beading.

This program intrigued me. This was another opportunity to experiment with the healing power of encounters. There was also the element of prevention. As a mother, citizen and parent of a murdered child, I was driven to work at prevention and safety of our vulnerable.

Plus – now that there was a suspect in our own case – someone accused in Candace's murder – I had a victim-offender battle of my own filled with issues that I needed to work out.

Suddenly, I had a personal need to know everything there was to know about these co-dependent, violent, often snarky, thundering offender clouds.

The pilot project program would include a dedicated, committed group of offenders who had volunteered for the program and a group of community members. We would begin creating healthy group dynamics by holding biweekly meetings with the inmates and separate monthly meetings with the community members. Then we would bring the two groups together so that they could meet. This would initiate the second half of the program – community members coaching the inmates on a creative path of redemption by designing beaded bracelets or jewelry that could be sold.

Beading is known to be a therapeutic activity that relieves stress – a soothing distraction. If we did this right, beading could be a productive way to pass the time and could even become a way to raise money.

Beading has always had amazing cross-cultural, cross-religious, cross-creative appeal.

The jewelry was to be sold to the wider community to raise money for a charitable organization.

The dialogues were amazing. We introduced a kind of Socratic dialogue model. Socrates believed that people are smarter in dialogue and interaction with others than when they are by themselves.

We believed that too. We would begin the dialogues by asking questions – simple ones at first – then move to universal questions such as "What is justice?" However, we never expected to agree on the answers.

But we trusted the process, and it worked. We were never sure where the wisdom would come from. Sometimes it was the community members who astounded us with their insight and original thinking, and sometimes it was the inmates.

In the end, the inmates were trained in jewelry-making by three professional beaders from the community. The community members were to encourage and coach them through the process.

All of the jewelry was worth celebrating – some inmates showed exceptional talent.

I remember our beginnings.

As we entered the large hall, C-16, and started to talk to the seven men who had self-selected to be part of our Paying Forward Project, I really wondered what we had to offer them.

A soft-spoken man sat beside me. He introduced himself as Tom. He looked more like a computer programmer – someone who should have been in an office behind a computer screen – than a prisoner sitting beside a tattooed, former gang member.

We had informally been told that he was on the edge – suicidal – and that he needed our group. He exuded and expressed dismal hopelessness that was reflected in his eyes – full of despair. "I'll never get out," he said. "Even if I serve my time, they hate me too much."

I glanced around the circle. Everyone seemed to agree with him. At this time, I had no idea what crime he had committed.

"I don't blame them," he continued. "But that wasn't me who really did that. I was high on drugs. I was mentally ill. It wasn't me."

Then about the third visit in, he told us that he had been asked to give a presentation at a workshop for training police recruits. "They want to know how I did it," he said.

"Why don't you do it?" we asked him. "It's an opportunity for you to do something good...to give back...."

He shook his head. "Never."

Over the next months, he would talk about the assignment apprehensively, always vowing that he would not even entertain the idea. He believed that the police would just use it against him, as everyone else had used his story against him. We kept encouraging him to keep his options open. More than that, we began to enjoy him in the group discussions. He would sit quietly in the background and then, when the talking piece came to him, he would articulate the theme in a way that filled us with admiration. He was astute, insightful – yet so completely without hope.

A year later, I was describing the dreadful sand storm I had encountered on my drive to Stony – an unusual occurrence that reminded me of pictures I had seen of the Dirty Thirties.

"I saw it," he said. There was a soft glow about him.

"How?" Even as I was describing the scene, I had realized the inmates' pain in not seeing anything outside of those impenetrable walls.

"I was outside."

I looked at him in disbelief.

"Yes, I was outside of these walls. I went downtown to give my presentation."

He was reluctant to go into details, but I gathered that he had held the audience of police officers spellbound for three hours as he told it all. I could tell by his demeanor that it had gone well for them – and for him.

"Best of all," he added, "I thought I would ride downtown with my nose pressed to the window, wanting it all – as I always had. I dreaded most the wanting it all and knowing that I would never have it again." He paused – his eyes full of peace. Something I had

174

not seen there before. "I didn't want it. I saw it for what it was. I was completely detached. I am free of it."

His values had changed – extrinsic to intrinsic. Huge.

He was now sitting in prison, a free man.

In group, as he described it again, he continually expressed his gratitude that it had been the program, our constant encouragement, our belief in him, and our challenges, that had given him the courage to do it.

This was the man who had gone on a seven-year crime spree involving robberies, break-ins, and a hostage-taking. It is no small accomplishment to pull off fifteen armed robberies, nine armored car heists, eight break-ins, one hostage-taking, as well as shooting three people (including two police officers).

He was taking ecstasy, marijuana, cocaine, morphine, and LSD. Desperation leads to desperate actions. I believe that our group conversations and dynamics addressed that inner desperation of loneliness that allowed him to gain the courage to do the right thing.

This one experience and personal accomplishment alone, I think, validates the program.

However, the beading had exceptional side benefits.

One inmate stated, "I needed to be in a positive space to bead. We're in lockdown, and I had to spend hours inside my cell. I would start beading and before I knew it, three hours had gone by. It made the lockdown a bit easier to deal with."

We called it Stepping Stones Jewelry Creations. The sales of jewelry amounted to $4,000 that was donated to the Candace Derksen Fund that had been set up at The Winnipeg Foundation.

After each year of the beading project, we brought in well-known speakers that had been victimized.

I knew that the storytelling would be powerful – just as it had been through the *Pathways* stories. I think it was a good experience for all of the speakers because we did really pamper them when they were with us. We didn't want to make them feel used. It was for their healing as well.

175

During this time, I was also meeting with a group of parents of murdered children in my home.

It was a time of hearing stories – and appreciating stories.

I would hear the story of the victims on Thursday. Monday, I would hear the stories of the inmates and community members.

At one point, I compared the conversations between the two groups. I actually felt the outside group – the victims of murder – were the angriest. They were so lost – without resources – trying to make sense of it.

The inmates were rested, eager, and well-nourished. But they lacked freedom, choices, and fresh views.

In all of this, I was learning that what worked for victims might not work for offenders. Victims were healed through their storytelling.

Public storytelling wasn't necessarily good for offenders. In our group, there were at least two inmates whose stories were published. It locked them into the criminal story, solidifying their identity.

And when they did tell their own stories to others, no matter how much they tried, they instinctively rationalized their crimes – or so it was perceived by those who were listening. Rationalizing murder is never acceptable.

Yet – the inmates need to process their own victimization stories. They, too, need to find their way back to value and redemption. I believe for that to happen they too need a very safe place.

The Paying Forward Project offered them a way to do just that. In talking about the beading project – and in the selling of the jewelry – the inmates were growing a new story – an acceptable story.

I believe for there to be true reconciliation the story of redemption needs to equal the story of the crime. Whether we want to admit it or not, the moral code written on our hearts is a life for a life. We can take the high road and fill in the gaps of justice with love, but the inherent social justice requires a kind of symbolic equity.

There is no equity in someone taking a life and then spending the rest of their life in jail – doing nothing and living off society.

But what if that life behind bars were able to tell a story of penance and regret – would the time be better served? And what if the story of redemption were told in beads rather than in words? Would it satisfy the need to prove its remorse?

If they couldn't express themselves in words, could they express themselves in beads? Everyone knows a churning cloud cannot bead. A raging, mean-spirited cloud cannot string a fragile bracelet together. It cannot choose colors that will harmonize and express peace and goodwill.

Perhaps a simple bracelet might be the best apology.

It might – that was our experiment.

Later on, I watched my daughter, who said she had no words, use crocheting as a creative means to tell the trial story. She sought special permission to bring a crochet hook into the courtroom to crochet disks.

She crocheted during the entire proceedings, choosing a color of wool that reflected her feelings at the moment. She used beige for boring, red for anger, and black for sadness. At the end of each day, she had a circular story, which later became part of a beautiful art installation that told the entire story of the trial at one glance. Instant gratification – profound and explicit.

Beadwork took time, humility, patience, and precision. The finished product could be jewelry, but it wouldn't have to be. It could take any form of art the inmate wanted. Just imagine twenty-five years expressed in beadwork!

In the present system, we force prisoners to sit in their cells with no form of expression, with no means of telling us what is going on in their hearts. We give them no tools to tell us if they are truly remorseful.

Could beading be the path to redemption? It was for one of our group. Tom was moved to minimum – and he deserved to be. Not soon after, he was released.

Chapter 19
JUSTICE

On the first day of the preliminary hearing, we woke up to the rumblings of a summer thunderstorm as fierce as anyone could imagine. Flashes of lightning, cracks of thunder startled us over and over again. It was an eerie summer version of the storm that had come on the day we had buried Candace.

Again the outside storm mirrored my own emotions.

A few weeks prior, my sister, Luella, and her husband, Jake Wiebe, had called from British Columbia. They were preparing to drive to Winnipeg in their camper van to join us for the preliminary. They had parked their Roadtrek van on our driveway.

I remember rushing out of the door that morning – anxious beyond reason – and saying, "We can take our car. It's probably easier to park in the Convention Centre with it. But for that, we will have to move your Roadtrek, Jake."

Then I stopped – there, standing in our driveway, was a home away from home!

"Oh, Jake, can we use your Roadtrek? It is a godsend…."

He was so proud to drive us there.

It worked perfectly. Because of their out-of-town license, they were given a tourist pass to park on the lovely legislative building grounds adjacent to the courthouse – which we used as a gathering place for family and friends whenever there was a pause in the proceedings. One day at noon, my sister even cooked corn-on-the-cob, fresh from Altona, for all of us – the perfect comfort food for us at that moment.

We used the Roadtrek for the entire time they were with us – three weeks.

This experience alone was enough to convince us that there was a need for a house – an off-campus place to feel safe.

But it wasn't over.

Two years after the preliminary hearing, the actual trial began – January 17, 2011 – exactly twenty-six years to the day that Candace's body was found. It lasted five weeks.

That first day was very formal. The Judge opened the trial proceedings with an official pronouncement of the charge. "…is being charged with first-degree murder," he said solemnly.

The jury looked as if they too felt they were in school, having their duties and task at hand outlined. The reporters had taken their places. There was a sketch artist at the left of the courtroom using very fast strokes. It looked as if he was sketching the jury members, using a tissue to smear and an eraser to smudge his charcoal lines. He also used different colored pencils to shade his illustration.

It was now official. Everything said and done in the courtroom could be publicized.

The Judge began the trial with instructions and general information for the jury.

Then the Assistant Prosecutor outlined the case in a narrative style, telling the official story of Candace's abduction and subsequent murder.

He ended with a solemn charge of his own. "It is our duty to ensure the right person is charged for the right offense."

Then the arguments began. In many ways it reminded me of a tournament in the Middle Ages – the challengers riding towards each other, touching their shields to begin the fight.

When the ceremony was over, the jousting began in earnest, with the combatants trying to strike their opponents in the head. It was surreal. If both stood firm, and there was a draw, the lances shattered.

But if the horse did not swerve and the lances did not break, and their aim was true, they could deliver the mortal wound – the fatal blow to the argument.

Not only were the Defence and Crown jousting – there was another combat. It was as if the dark clouds of the victim and offender were having their own staged tournament above – mimicking what was happening on the floor beneath them.

My eyes drifted to the throne-like wooden chair, majestic and old, placed at the very back, behind the Judge's desk and chair – empty, as if ceremonially symbolizing the presence of the Queen herself and embodying all of her authority. I could visualize Queen Elizabeth there, tiara on her silver hair, dressed in royal blue, regal, demanding pomp and ceremony and presiding over it.

We had named Candace after Queen Candace of Ethiopia. Now to hear Candace's name and hear her death described in this regal presence was a kind of poetic justice that moved me. I could feel Candace in the room.

At the back of the room, separated by a brass rail, was our visitors' gallery with olive green, leather theater chairs. The walls were marble. The ceiling was ornately covered in gold leaf stencil and carved moldings.

And there was Candace in her chair, queen of the moment, redeemed...honored.

I think it was this regal setting juxtaposed with the descriptions of the abandoned shed where Candace was murdered that shifted my world view so vividly and shook my emotions.

Unexpectedly, during this time I received an email from defense lawyer, Alan Libman, asking me for breakfast. We had never talked, except at the board meetings. I was nervous. Lawyers make me nervous.

We met at the Original Pancake House on Pembina.

After a bit of chitchat, he laid out his agenda. "I think you are discouraged about the house." He was reading my mind. "I think Candace House has got to happen, and I want to help you."

He said it with such pure conviction, I remember just staring at him.

Surprised that he was so concerned – so interested.

Everyone else who had encouraged me usually had obvious motivation.

But a defense lawyer? A well-positioned lawyer?

He seemed to sense my disbelief.

"I see what victims go through," he said.

Then I realized that he too was in the business of defending, helping and making victims. He was in the thick of the battle.

I then took him seriously. If he thought it was a good idea – maybe it had validity.

He wanted a plan.

I gave him a plan – and the House dream was in motion again.

It wasn't difficult to see the need for a house as we continued with the trial.

The house could be a place for validation. There is something very demeaning about attending a trial based on one's loved one. I could not believe how the justice system ignored us – the parents. The victims! I was invisible – always had been – so it wasn't that hard. The Judge would come in – address the accused, the Crowns, the Defense, and the jury members. And then they would start.

In this day and age, we are used to being greeted at Walmart – or wherever we go. Attending court was like going to the grandest party, the most official meeting in the nation, and being strategically ignored by the host. I estimated that I had been in and out of courtrooms close to seventy days – a sum total of twelve weeks – which makes it three months of living in the courtroom. Not once were we included.

Thank goodness I had shored myself up with ways of building my social equity by blogging and by staging and orchestrating social interactions at the end of the day or at least at the end of the trial.

But what if I had been alone? As so many are. I had a home to gather people. What if I didn't have a home? I would need a home – a house.

The house could be a place of much-needed privacy and safety. There is something very unsafe about the courthouse. A courtroom is a place of constant battle. Under the veneer of etiquette and politeness, there is a tournament going on.

Lawyers refer to each other as "my learned friend" and refer to solicitors, police officers, and court staff simply as "my friend." They all refer to the Judge as "your Honor" or at least "Sir" or "Madam."

The lawyers never enter or leave a courtroom without bowing to the Judge. It is said that it is not the Judge they are bowing to but the "presence" of the Queen. So the Queen, in essence, is also there in the middle of the jousting, the fight for justice.

Therefore, victims need a place to be real – to vent, to rage, to pout, or just to hide. They need to have a place for private conversations and a place to just let down their guard.

Even the washrooms are public places. Although I personally didn't have a member of the offender family come into the washroom when I was there, I was always on guard. One never knows. The house place would need a private washroom. When in trauma, we need one little cubicle where we can sit to have our ugly cry and take care of stress-related irritable bowel syndrome.

The house could offer a place to meet the professionals.

Various meetings need different levels of privacy and comfort.

There needs to be a place to simply eat. Often there are court groupies that come around in the public cafeteria and want to befriend the newsworthy victims. I was so vulnerable in that. It's hard to say no to a stranger who wants just a few moments of your time. When everyone is watching, the possibilities of misunderstanding and embarrassment are multiplied.

There needs to be a place for family time – a smaller room for those intimate conversations that preserve family unity.

Lawyers do have wonderful offices with lovely boardrooms, but that place is on their turf – in their comfort zone. Again, no quick access to coffee – or any of the amenities of home that a traumatized body needs.

In the beginning, the police came to our home – and we had no option but to invite them into our lives at the most inopportune times. It would be good to have a choice.

The house could be a place to meet the media.

The media isn't allowed to conduct interviews in the Law Courts – which is a good thing. But meeting them outside, during a Winnipeg winter – as we did – was not pleasant. Makes for a great story – and color – but it is not conducive as a place to answer serious life questions with the traffic roaring in the background, people waving…and all of that.

The house could be a spiritual place.

There wasn't a place to bow our heads in public! I remember how – during one victim-offender encounter in Edmonton – we had to do a quick smudge in the middle of a parking lot. We need privacy and comfort to talk to our God – especially at a time when we can do with the courage, strength, wisdom of talking and communication with a higher power.

The house could be a place to nap.

Not to stay the night – there are hotels and homes for that. Spending time in a courtroom is exhausting! I know one woman who had spent so much time in the court halls that she fell asleep on a bench in the hallway. She was rudely asked to leave because her disheveled appearance gave the impression that she was a vagrant.

The house could be a place to ask dumb questions.

The constant issue throughout our thirty-five-year process is how culturally different the justice system is compared to normal life. Vocabulary, systems, expectations, rules – everything is different. Even the people who inhabit that world have a different way of thinking. For the unaccustomed victim, it can be quite intimidating. Yet, it is an opportunity for great learning. But to do that one needs to engage and have a safe place to learn, access the resources needed and ask the dumb questions.

It's also known that it is information – and access to it – that brings healing to people who are traumatized by crime. They need a resource place where they can access information and ask what they might feel to be their "dumb" questions.

The house could offer a place to park.

There is no greater stressor for someone living in the suburbs than to think about parking downtown. The expense is also unreal – especially if one has adult children that need to attend. Transportation needs are important.

The house could offer a place to wait.

There is a lot of waiting that happens during the justice process. One inevitable time is the period when the jury is deliberating before they come to a verdict.

The house would offer a place for someone to deal with those jousting clouds that didn't end their fighting when they left the courtroom.

I'll never forget that day. Just before the summations, an author friend of mine came into Courtroom 230, a little out of breath.

"I just had to buy this for you," she said, as she handed me a white rose.

I gasped. "Did you read this morning's blog?"

She nodded.

I instantly felt contrite. That morning before driving to the courthouse, I had published a rather self-absorbed blog.

I think I might need a special bouquet of flowers when the jury returns with their verdict....

And now she was standing there with a rose!

"Yes. I wanted to get you a rose, so on my way here, I stopped by a florist and they had this one white rose left, but no vial of water to keep it fresh. I took it. I didn't want to miss anything so I don't know how it will keep."

I hugged her.

Not wanting the rose to be seen by the jury as giving some kind of message, I simply stuck it into my daughter's crocheting bag behind my chair – out of sight, but not out of mind.

As we were going for lunch, my daughter noticed the rose in her bag. "Should I take it with me to the room?" she asked.

We had been given a special room on the fourth floor just for the family. This had been one of the developments that I had noticed over the years – the system was listening to our requests. It was a tiny room.

Should I take this rose to our room? "Not yet." For some felt reason, I wanted the rose to stay with me in the courtroom for the entire time we were listening to the summations and Judge's charge. I wanted its short life to mean something.

For the rest of the day, I laid it down on an unused chair to the side. At the end of the long day after the two summaries and the Judge's charge to the jury, I noticed the rose still on the chair, looking completely wilted. It had spent its life to comfort me. It was done.

Not willing to part with it, I took it to our fourth-floor family room, poured water into a tiny coffee cup, and propped it up against a cup dispenser at the back of the kitchenette counter, vaguely wondering if it would escape the night cleaning crew.

After the court was dismissed, we debriefed with the Crowns. They had no predictions. They had practiced law long enough to never second-guess a jury, they said.

Now was the time of waiting. Even though nothing was happening, we still needed to be there – no more than twenty minutes away, just in case they came down with a verdict.

Thursday morning, the first thing I noticed when we returned to our tiny room was that the white rose had fully revived. I touched the cheek of the flower petal to express my gratitude, to love it. Not only had it survived, but it also seemed to have grown in its beauty, opening slowly in radiant splendor. It gave me such comfort. I stared at it for quite a while.

Why was it so alive?

Prepared to wait for a long time, we settled in on the fourth floor, in the new part of the building with warm beige rugs, trendy purple couches, and blonde oak trim. The older part of the building, marbled and ornate with wooden benches, had an entirely different feel to it.

But the new building has definite living possibilities. It's actually quite a nice place for a regular family gathering. We opened our tiny victim room, which was furnished with a sofa and easy chairs, to all our friends.

It soon started to feel like one of those extended family gatherings – entertaining in your own living room.

I remember one moment when I looked around. From where I sat, I could see the older ones lounging on the sofas against the far wall, talking with each other. Across the hall, there were four young adults, our adult children with their adult cousins, playing Dutch Blitz in an interview room. A delightful toddler was crawling down the hallway, a young mother watching over him. The young father was sitting between his uncle and another friend comparing BlackBerrys.

There were two more adult cousins in the little family room with the tiny kitchenette counter, eating, and reading. It all felt so warm and cozy. The time slipped easily through our fingers.

Later that evening, I took a call on my cellphone and wandered away from the visitors toward the front of the court building. The north wall was all glass – four-story-high windows.

The call was David, Candace's friend. "Notice the blizzard," he said. "Does it remind you of anything?"

I looked out. The weather had changed drastically. When we had driven here in the morning, it had been quite pleasant and warm, at least for February in Winnipeg. Now a cold front had blown in. It was storming.

It felt all so familiar standing there in front of those huge windows watching the snow blow off the top of the building.

I am reminded again that this isn't a simple family gathering being held in a strange place. We are waiting for a very important verdict.

There is a fierce debate going on at the far end of the building where a jury of twelve is cloistered away, discussing in detail all the evidence that they have heard during the last five weeks.

The questions seem almost interchangeable with the ones I was faced with twenty-six years ago, when it all started, on a stormy winter night. "Where are you, Candace?" It was a long, lonely night as I prayed the question, watching the storm moving through our city.

Now I stand at the window again, watching the tumultuous wind whip up the snow into a frenzy. Now the question is: What is the verdict, Candace? It is another long, lonely night as I pray the question.

The battle was raging inside me. It was also raging out there in the dark clouds, in Room 230 with the jurors, and in the hearts of my friends and family who had joined us.

Around 8:00 p.m. Friday evening, there were "rumblings" from the journalists that a verdict was coming down.

Odia was crocheting in red.

We made our way down to the second floor of the old building, to Room 230.

There was a flurry of activity with everyone texting and making phone calls. People were already gathering when we got to the room, standing excitedly in the hall outside the courtroom – media, police, family, and friends – chatter, laughter, excitement.

It was odd to be gathering in Room 230 on a Friday evening at 8:30 p.m. The most unexpected people appeared, coming down the long hallway – a little disheveled, a little nervous, hushed and concerned. It was like a surprise party but without celebration – only relief and anticipation.

When the doors of the courtroom opened, we found our seats in the front row. There was a pleasant hum in the room until we heard the accused's leg shackles rattling at 8:50 p.m. He was dressed in his suit. The reason for our gathering was not a good one. It was sobering to think what lay in the balance for the accused – a life in prison, perhaps, or freedom. The energy left the room when he took his place in the prisoner's box. I started to hear sniffles.

And that's when the panic set in for me – this was the moment we had all been waiting for. This was the end of knowing if he was guilty or not.

If I was feeling like this – what about the rest of my family? We had not been able to touch base. For the last three days, it seemed as if we had been all floating about, never centered enough to talk to each other. Never really asking the question, "How are you doing?" Especially during this last long day of waiting, we had all separated to be with our age group.

My children and their spouses had hung out with their cousins and friends. Even though we had been together, we hadn't talked.

Then I remembered the metaphor that we had chosen to not only remind ourselves to accept the process but also to calm ourselves, to center ourselves. It was to see this entire court building as a sanctuary. We were not to see the courtroom as a place of judgment and justice but as a sanctuary – a temple of God. It was – perhaps – the holy of holies.

It had been interesting watching our son throughout the trial. Since he had never truly encountered Candace, he was learning about her first-hand now – and integrating it with what he was learning.

At that moment, as we readied ourselves to hear the verdict, I noticed that Syras had taken his shoes off already – so had Natasha…. I looked back – so had Odia and Larry. We had all taken our shoes off.

Without a word, we understood each other's heart – and we smiled at each other – tentatively…. We were all in solidarity. I didn't have to worry about them.

The clouds were poised.

At 9:00 p.m. the Judge arrived and looked over the room – a little surprised by the large number of people present. He made some remarks to the gallery about the reason we were gathered. He said that the jury had worked hard and had deliberated long and hard and that we must respect their decision, whatever it was. "If anyone cannot keep their emotions in check, please leave. Please no outburst in the court this evening."

Then the jury filed in and took their places. It was different seeing them in the evening. The windows were dark. The Judge looked weary.

Everyone looked tired of waiting.

Then, finally, juror number seven stood to give the verdict. He was the tall man at the gallery end of the second row. His hands were shaking as he held the verdict.

The foreman read from his paper. "First-degree – not guilty."

I didn't breathe.

"Second-degree – guilty."

It took me a while to process the words. He was guilty – but not of first-degree murder. What did that mean? How had they arrived at that decision? That hadn't actually been one of the options in the decision tree.

At first, it all seemed contradictory.

But then he summarized it again. "Guilty of second-degree murder," he said. It was the startling announcement.

Guilty!

That's all that mattered. It was over.

Whether it was first-degree or second-degree murder wasn't important to me.

Relief!!! Gratitude! It was over. I was now free of it!

Just to make sure everyone was in agreement, the Defense Counsel polled everyone. Each juror stood up individually and said, "Guilty." Juror number ten seemed upset.

All twelve jurors concurred that the accused was guilty.

Then the thought – the word that was freeing me was now robbing him of his freedom and sending him to prison.

The Judge began to summarize as he addressed the jury. Guilty of second-degree murder was a sentence to life imprisonment.

The Judge allowed the jury to consult in private and give their recommendation about the sentence and their recommended period of parole ineligibility.

He gave them a ten-minute recess. Without speaking, we went around the room and silently hugged everyone there. I would also like to have hugged every one of my friends and family who weren't able to come to be there with us during that moment. I wanted to hug everyone who had said a prayer for us during the last twenty-six years, sent a note, gave chocolate, sent us a poem, a word, sat with us, or gave us some small gesture of support. I was so grateful to them all. Without them, I know we couldn't have endured all of those long, dark years of not knowing.

When the jury returned, they respectfully declined to give a recommendation regarding the length of the sentence or the period of parole ineligibility.

Then the Judge again cautioned the jury about breaking their oath of confidentiality. He told them again that the jury room was a private and sacred space. "In the Criminal Code, it is an offense to disclose any information about your discussions, whatever opinions are expressed. Nothing is to be discussed." He thanked them for their services in coming to a decision in a very difficult and emotional trial.

The jousting was over – the dark court clouds dissipated....

All we wanted was to find each other and be together as a family again.

But first, we had to pack up all of our things in the family room. It's amazing how many personal belongings we had brought into the Law Courts Building.

While everyone was waiting at the elevator to go down, I did what I always do when I leave a motel room. I do a final sweep of the room to see what my children have left behind. Even though they are all adults now, it is a hard habit to break.

The room was empty except for two garbage bins, filled to the brim with all kinds of cartons for take-out food. The chairs were a little askew, so I straightened them.

Then I noticed the single rose standing on the window sill. It had been mysteriously moved from behind the cup dispenser to the window that faced the Remand Centre, still in the tiny cup of water. It stood tall, regal, as only a long-stemmed white rose can do – a lonely gesture of love against the dark night.

For one moment, I wondered about taking it with me. The duffel bags were already packed and gone. I had nothing to wrap the rose in. Without protection, it would never survive the freezing temperatures of the night.

But I still couldn't throw it away. More than ever, I now needed it close to me for comfort. I grabbed it and headed for the doors.

The journalists were waiting for us. It seemed a million lights started flashing all at once as we opened the front doors of the Law Courts Building.

What a surprise!

I know I should have expected it, but there is really nothing to prepare oneself for a moment like that.

They asked us questions, and, as usual, I fumbled for the right words. Then one of the reporters asked me, "Why are you holding a white rose?"

I looked down. Yes – I was holding the rose.

White rose!

Should I tell them? Should I tell them that I was cleaning up the room, grabbing what was left behind, and then simply forgot to pack it? I was holding a rose but it could have been anything that had been left behind. Yet now – holding the white rose – it seemed so appropriate for the moment. I had been so worried about finding the right words – the right sound bite for that impossible moment – and there it was in my hand.

A white rose is worth a thousand words.

As it turned out, I kept that rose. It hung it on the corner of my dresser mirror.

Symbolic of the entire process.

It was white, exhausted, dried, and lifeless but still beautiful.

Chapter 20
EXPERT

"Congratulations!" it read. "Your application to speak at TEDx Manitoba 2012 has been accepted!"

I hadn't applied to do any such thing. "Scam!" I thought as I deleted it.

Once the trial was over, as we plunged back into our lives, one of the first things I had to deal with was the long backlog of emails that seemed dated and irrelevant.

But a few days later, I received another email from a respected well-known pastor here in the city. She was a kind, generous, articulate, beautiful woman that I had admired from afar.

"Why haven't you answered?" she asked in her email. "I nominated you as a speaker for the next TEDx Manitoba talks and they tell me that you haven't responded. I was hoping to give you a platform to talk about forgiveness. I think you have something valuable to say. Why don't you want to do this?"

I quickly googled TEDx and realized it wasn't a scam at all. This nomination was, in fact, a great honor.

I answered immediately. "I will do it. I don't know what it is – but I will do it."

She said that the committee had been very receptive to her nomination and was interested in my stance on forgiveness. My nomination had passed without question. I couldn't help but remember twenty-six years ago when everyone was so skeptical, and even offended, by our choice to forgive.

Shortly after, I met the provincial Minister of Justice at a gala, and he too asked me when I was going to write the book on forgiveness. "People need to know," he said. He brought it up twice that evening.

And there were other overtures as well. It seemed as if everyone wanted to know.

Not only was I now being accepted, I was suddenly being asked as an expert. Instead of defending, disguising, hiding, or apologizing for our forgiveness – I was being asked to explain it.

Apparently, the intense media coverage had revealed that after twenty-six years of living with the unsolved murder of our daughter and then enduring the rigors of the trial, we were still together. Cliff and I had emerged from the courthouse arm and arm together. Our children, who were visible in the background, had matured, married and were also emotionally healthy.

As for us – we were quite oblivious of the images we were projecting.

We had expected everyone to be interested in the court proceedings. What we didn't realize was that they were just as interested in our personal processes because of our choice to forgive. Would it hold?

They had concluded it did. Now they were interested in the process. They were interested in forgiveness. They now wanted an explanation.

And I didn't have a clue.

I really didn't.

The spotlight felt demanding and invasive. It was also attracting a whole new set of clouds from my childhood. Having been brought up invisible, I had visibility issues.

It wasn't only the public that intimidated me, it was the new bank of clouds watching me as I was filled with insecurities and negative self-talk.

However, the need to define forgiveness was not new.

I remember being on this exact quest before – to define forgiveness.

I had just started my program, Victims' Voice, and was looking for words and ideas to help crime victims heal. I thought a theological understanding of the word forgiveness might form the basis of our mandate. If I could only find the right definition, I could fashion the perfect sound bite to describe our program. It was all about branding. I could then develop a wonderful brochure.

Around this time, I was invited to a conference in Washington, D.C. – the Theological Forum on Crime Victims and the Church, a theological and practical exploration of victimization, justice, evil and forgiveness, organized by Neighbors Who Care and Prison Fellowship Ministries in October 1997.

It was a two-day meeting of learned, hand-picked theologians from across the United States. These were amazingly articulate scholars presenting papers that were later published in a book.

But, as the meeting proceeded, I became quite anxious knowing that, even though the words were beautiful, there was nothing in them for me personally. Nothing practical. There was nothing for the group of crime victims at home who were awaiting my return. At least nothing understandable.

Half an hour before we were to leave, someone dared to ask, "Have we defined forgiveness yet?"

The room was quiet. Absolute silence. Then there were some valiant attempts to summarize the discussions, but from where I was sitting nothing made sense. Their words fell short. There was huge, visible disappointment in the entire group as we sat there at the end of day, fumbling for words. We finally left – with a sense of not being finished.

The next morning, it was still dark when I climbed into the back seat of the taxi at 5:00 a.m. feeling miserable, dreading going home and having to report that I was returning with nothing but a growing sense of futility.

I was also slightly annoyed with myself for not taking into account the long ride to the airport when I had booked a flight home at such a ridiculous hour of the morning.

"Good morning," the driver said cheerfully, as I settled back into the seat, grumpily.

The driver didn't seem to notice my mood and chattered pleasantly about all kinds of things, the hotel, the weather, but I didn't respond. I was offering the occasional one-syllable answer, but nothing to encourage him.

Finally, he paused. "I'm sorry for jabbering on and on like this," he said softly, "but you are the first sober fare I've had all night."

Immediately I felt dreadful. We had at least a forty-five-minute drive to airport, so I apologized and told him that I hadn't had my coffee.

He nodded. He said he understood. Apparently, my accent gave me away, so he asked me a little bit about Canada.

When he found out I worked with homicide issues, he seemed pleasantly interested – even open. So, I dared to ask him why the city of Washington, where he lived, had the highest rate of murder in all of North America.

He fell silent for a long moment. Then he said, "My brothers are still angry because of those years of slavery, the racism in this country, and the poverty. This anger shows itself in violence."

He went on and on about it all. Even though he was identifying with his people, describing great sorrow and pain, I couldn't help but notice that he spoke with no anger and absolutely no bitterness. In fact, in the dark, he seemed to glow with some inner joy and sunshine.

I couldn't resist. I asked him the burning question. "I can tell you that you aren't angry. Why not?"

Without missing a beat, he said. "I believe in forgiveness."

"What of forgiveness?" I asked tentatively.

Without any further prompting, he talked about forgiveness with an eloquence I had never heard before or since. He talked about the beauty of being set free, of letting go of the past, embracing the moment, and anticipating the future. He talked enthusiastically about the benefits, the joys and the victory.

By this time, the sun was beginning to rise. It seemed so symbolic of what was happening in the car. The light was flooding in.

In simple terms, he was able to describe what those learned scholars had failed to do in the previous two days. He not only described forgiveness – he radiated the word.

By the time I reached the airport, I felt like a new person.

I decided then and there that forgiveness doesn't need to be defined, it just needs to be lived and felt.

Over the years, I had shelved my desire to define forgiveness. I thought it was a coping word, a resilience word. The definitions I had used were inadequate and dismissive and complicated.

I was at a loss to know how to address the word. Eventually, I had decided that it was impossible to deal with. One doesn't have to define it – one only needs to use it and live it.

Was I now the taxi driver to those around me, somehow radiating the power of forgiveness? Were they asking, "What of forgiveness?" I wished I had taped him.

I could have used his words now, facing the daunting task of a structured TEDx talk – a twenty-minute talk – under the spotlights – entitled "When Polarity in Forgiveness Happens." This not only needed to be described in a compelling narrative, it needed to be logical as well.

Desperate, I looked at my research. I had my *Fifteen Elements*. This was a tried and true list of all the issues I had faced. This was one side of forgiveness, the ugly side. Then I got the idea that I could describe forgiveness if I just somehow applied my list of fifteen elements to forgiveness. I would just apply a "let go" to each of them.

Somehow, I pulled it together.

It seemed well received.

I was so relieved. It didn't feel comfortable. Besides, it was finished. I could now just point everyone to the presentation that was available online.

A few months later, I received another email.

My name is Malcolm Gladwell, and I'm a writer in New York. I would love to come to Winnipeg and interview you for a book I'm writing. I have been reading about the story of your daughter and have been very moved by it.

I don't know if you are still giving interviews, but if you are, do let me know. I would be happy to come to Winnipeg.

Cheers, M.

I answered. "Are you the Malcolm Gladwell, staff writer for *The New Yorker* who has written *The Tipping Point* (2000) and *Blink: The Power of Thinking without Thinking* (2005)?"

He answered that yes – he was the same person. Would I consent to the interview?

I had just read the *Tipping Point* and raved about it to my friends. Was I being set up?

We set a time – and I never quite believed he would show up.

He did! He came to Winnipeg to interview me on June 30, 2012. He actually came to our door, and we sat down to talk for two hours in our backyard gazebo.

He was incredible. His questions were probing, insightful and yet affirming. He had studied my writings – and I felt as if he was someone who really understood me.

Basically, I think he wanted to know if my forgiveness was real.

Apparently, some people thought it impossible to forgive after the murder of a child.

He included our story in his book *David and Goliath: Underdogs, Misfits, and the Art of Battling Giants*, a non-fiction book, published by Little, Brown, and Company on October 1, 2013 – the month that the Court of Appeal reversed the trial decision.

Word got out that Gladwell had come to see me – which added to the intrigue.

I was being asked more frequently and more seriously to describe forgiveness. I was being studied.

Frankly, I became curious as well.

What had started this journey? Why had I started this journey? And why was it so much part of me?

Then I remembered the moment when I made the concept of forgiveness my own.

After graduating from Bethany Bible School, Cliff followed me to Vancouver where we found work, married and set up our first home in a basement suite.

There had been adjustments for both of us – some difficult. We were both country bumpkins moving to a huge, sophisticated city. We were enjoying it all, lunching in Stanley Park, haunting Gastown and zooming down the freeway to visit my parents. Wondering about each other, and wondering what we would do with our lives.

In the middle of all of these transitions, I found a book by one of my favorite authors – Lloyd C. Douglas. I had read all of his books in our church library: *The Magnificent Obsession, The Robe, The Big Fisherman* – some that were made into lavish Technicolor movies – blockbusters in their time.

The book I found was entitled *White Banners* – which wasn't at all like his other books. I couldn't believe it was written by the same author. This one was about a woman – and about pacifism.

Up till now, my father and my Mennonite culture had placed the belief of non-resistant pacifism in the context of war. For my father, war had been an issue that challenged those in his age group, divided them and made them all experts on the subject.

None of that applied to me.

But this book placed all of that right in the middle of my world – a woman's world.

I had read this book…as an impressionable young woman.

I had read it a long time ago. Now I wondered? What had it really said? Would it match the vivid memories that I still had of it – or had I imagined it all?

I ordered the book. Around this time, in the fall of 2013, my younger sister died, and my world was reeling again. I had spent some significant moments with Pat – and she had felt a little like Candace. I was going back in time.

I reread the book on the plane to her memorial on Vancouver Island, there and back. It was just as powerful as the first read and it healed me again.

Some of the issues were dated, but that didn't matter – it held the same sacred ability to influence me.

The setting was Indiana, in 1919. It begins on one cold and wintery day, when a woman, Hannah, knocks on the door of a financially struggling couple, Professor Paul Ward, and his wife Marcia, and their two children. Hannah endears herself to Marcia and begins to influence the home with her ideas and pearls of wisdom.

The couple doesn't know that she is living out an experiment. At least that's what I had named it in my mind.

The story is about how Hannah, whose father works for an estate owner, falls in love with the rich son, Phillip, who is dying. During his decline, she reads history books to him from which he forms a unique philosophy of life.

Phillip comes to the conclusion that war always brings about more destruction, poverty and mayhem. It is always unproductive. So, in his dying days, he explores a new way of thinking and living. He believes that if one has an enemy that does "steal or take something" it is counterproductive to fight and shame them. To dishonor someone is to create not only an enemy but another victim.

The better way is to relinquish and adhere to a non-combative lifestyle – choosing to honor everyone. Even those who war against and steal from us believe that we are either a threat or have something they want. We are targeted because we are the ones who are privileged and have the better ability to recover.

His main word is "adaption." The privileged, the ones who "have," need to see each conflict or injustice as a way of moving on and "adapting" to the loss, regrouping and trying again. In this way, each "loss" becomes an opportunity to learn to do it again, to recover from the loss and do it better. "Adaption." In other words, an injustice is an opportunity.

The hope is that those who live like this gain extraordinary wisdom and resilience.

Phillip's one regret is that he is dying and will never be able to test his hypothesis. Hannah offers to try it. He discourages her by saying it will be a very difficult life to live, but she determines to do it anyway. He dies.

Hannah lives on – and the book is about how she, in her own way, as a servant in a house, is constantly "letting go" – in other words, forgiving, and adapting to each new situation, bringing all the old learning to the new. She lives a non-combative, adjusting lifestyle – as a kind of experiment to see if it is viable.

Her life does turn out to be very difficult, but it is also rich, beautiful and full of drama.

After reading this book as a young woman, I remember deciding that I was going to be a Hannah. She appealed to me.

I probably also decided this because I am a hopeless romantic. I admired her enduring love – this was true love. Romance is the ultimate experiment.

Even though I wasn't always conscious of Hannah or the book, in hindsight, reading it again, I could see how it was in my unconscious…always present.

Every once in a while, a book comes along that defines you and changes your life forever. *White Banners* changed me. It had made me a believer in forgiveness and in a non-combative lifestyle.

And then, as can be expected, my living it out was not easy. When I suffered from postpartum depression after Odia was born, filled with resentment because I felt that I had lost out on the opportunity to go back to university after I had worked to support Cliff and his education, I experimented with forgiveness. Why was I sad? What did I have to let go of? How could I adapt?

My own father disappointed me and I had to forgive him – move on – which was in some ways the underlying reason Cliff and I moved to Winnipeg. In hindsight this was the best move we could have made.

Winnipeg is wonderful.

Adaption, moving, changing had worked for us on many levels.

Then I received a letter from another person.

I'm an editor.... I'm also a person, like you, who has faced murder in their family and home life....

The reason I tell you this, Wilma, is that your "When Polarity in Forgiveness Happens" is the most powerful set of teachings for our lives that I've ever found. Philip Yancey, who directed me to you, is an author of ours who has spoken on the "why" of suffering many times in his books; he has two new books coming out, one of which I understand will involve a filming session with you by one of our teams this summer.

This letter is about you and how you have helped so many, including writer Malcolm Gladwell, whose book and interview articles I have before me. I also am looking at your publications: Unsettled Weather, a workbook of seven sessions about how to forgive (Herald Press), Confronting the Horror: The Aftermath of Violence, the stages of crime elements that a crime victim will endure (Amity), Have You Seen Candace, the story of Candace and the agonizing search for your abducted daughter (Amity), and The Emerald Angel, a novel about a young girl and her attraction to her grandmother as a gifted caregiver (Herald Press).

I could not believe this....

This was an agent from Zondervan, HarperCollins Christian Publishing division. He came to visit on May 27, 2014, with a Philip Yancey film crew – hinting that he wanted a book on forgiveness from me.

By this time, I was in a panic.

I couldn't write a book on forgiveness with any kind of authority.

After he left, I ordered every book I could from Amazon on forgiveness – and started skimming all of them. I devoted a whole year to this research.

I was disappointed. A lot of the books centered on encouragement and inspiration. Most books centered on reconciliation with the "enemy," even promoting "love for the offender," which was not a bad thing. But I really didn't find anything substantial about forgiveness as a stand-alone method to deal with the aftermath of murder, especially in our case when the murderer is unknown. The definitions of forgiveness usually included ways to deal with complex relationships.

It was the concept of Hannah's "adaption" that was missing.

As I read the philosophy books about forgiveness, I was also surprised that the ancient philosophers such as Plato and Socrates didn't write about it or see value in it. It became viable only after Jesus came, as an example of a personal choice.

I did learn that forgiveness is innate. Apparently, even chimpanzees forgive. All social species have to learn to get along with each other and forgive constantly in many ways. We forgive automatically when someone steps on our toes – at least most of the time.

However, when the losses are substantial – irreplaceable – and the relinquishing of anger becomes seemingly impossible, we start to resist and fight for our rights. It requires a great deal of faith to believe that a life-threatening, permanent injustice can be turned into a positive, life-giving opportunity.

The editor did not give up on me as I struggled with the concept. He would occasionally write to ask me how it was coming along.

Finally, I went to our pastor at Soul Sanctuary – and asked if I could test my biblical and psychological ideas of forgiveness on a focus group.

I called it *Fierce Forgiveness* and ran it from September 16 to November 18, 2015. I was really looking for a definition that encompassed or captured everything I had learned.

After the focus group, I finally sent the editor an outline of all of my academic learnings. He was not impressed. Apparently, he didn't want my newly-acquired expertise. He wanted a book based on the fifteen "let go's" that I had developed from the *Fifteen Elements* as presented in the TEDx talk.

I finally shelved all of my learnings and submitted a simple outline of "letting go."

This led to a book assignment, *The Way of Letting Go,* with the first deadline February 16, 2016. Customarily, books are released exactly one year after signing.

That gave me time to work on the book, but also for the case to continue to work through the justice system. We were shocked when the "guilty" decision of the jury was overturned by the Court of Appeal of Manitoba which sent it to the Supreme Court of Canada. Surprised at every turn, we continued to follow the proceedings faithfully – even traveling to Ottawa as a family to attend the Supreme Court hearing.

A few months later we learned that they agreed with the decision of the Manitoba Court of Appeal and ordered a retrial. The dates of the retrial were set for January 16 to March 3, 2017.

And that was the concern – the book would be released during the retrial…. Horrors! I tried to talk to both the publisher and the Crown to lessen the impact of the collision between the book and trial, but I had little say or influence. I would just have to let it happen.

It all turned out.

We launched the book – and it had its own life. The editor was right. It was timely.

I was receiving amazing letters from all over the world.

I am from the United States. I am almost finished with your book, "The Way of Letting Go," and I am just blown away by the revelation and healing it has brought to me. The season I am in, it has been everything I needed and more.

I am a survivor of molestation, rape, abuse, childhood trauma in the home, suicide attempts.... the list goes on. Your book captivated me instantly and has quite honestly been the first book I have physically been able to read, in full, in over 13 years....

After reading it, I didn't feel crazy anymore.

It didn't end there. After the retrial, the accused was acquitted and released. It might not have been the outcome we expected, but by then we had "let go" of any expectations of a satisfactory ending. But at least it felt like an ending.

Then the media, CBC news, announced on October 17, 2019 that....

The man who spent a decade behind bars for the murder of Winnipeg teen Candace Derksen is suing the police and the Crown prosecutor's office for $8.5 million in damages, in what he calls a wrongful conviction.

The suit cites "negligent investigation, malicious prosecution, breach of his Charter rights and wrongful conviction."

It just wouldn't end. As long as the issues kept presenting themselves to us, it was hard to create closure. This justice-making process, which seemed to be a subplot in our lives, kept surprising us and continuing to involve us by putting our name into the media every time.

As far as we know, the suit remains before the courts.

And with each twist and turn, those stalking, dark clouds would appear – rubbing their hands with glee.

Chapter 21
PIXIE DUST

"Now is the time," she said sipping her tea. "It really is…."

"Why now?" I asked.

"Your trial has put you in the public eye and we need to take advantage of this moment to benefit all of us." Her brother had been murdered, and her trauma had been acute.

She proposed we meet regularly and start planning the Candace House in earnest.

Then her dear friend – a sophisticated, articulate and well-connected woman, whose son was murdered – stepped in to dream with us. After that – unknown to the other two – another came alongside me. She was a bundle of energy who later took the minutes and became the glue of the committee. Then, just as we were becoming formalized, another woman approached me, and I introduced her to the group. She was the perfect addition – elegant, mild-mannered yet passionate – who brought an aura of peace to us. Last, but certainly not least, was the wife of a journalist – who just sparkled.

Because some of these women worked in the Legislative Building, we were welcomed to meet there.

The Legislative Women were right. There is that opportune time to introduce a good initiative to solve a social problem. We had seen it with the swimming pool at Camp Arnes that had been introduced at the time of Candace's funeral. Child Find Manitoba had been introduced at the time of Candace's disappearance. Both had brought meaning to us as well as to the community.

Meaning was important to the healing process – to deal with the trauma. I knew that – but there was another reason…a lingering, lifetime reason….

Her insistent suggestion took me down memory lane – seven years ago – right after the accused had been charged with first degree murder. I flew to Calgary.

I was in an odd mood. I thought the charge would bring out the anger in me – which it did. It brought out that reptilian cloud which haunted me for a time until I resolved all those issues again. But the surprise was that it also brought out another cloud – a misty, less threatening cloud but one that surrounded me, trapped me and isolated me, making me feel very alone. Yet, because this cloud was less threatening – I could dismiss and mostly ignore it.

In any case, I had to honor an invitation to speak in Calgary – a commitment I had made a year earlier and now didn't have the heart to cancel – even though my life had changed so much since then.

I remember the day clearly.

The taxi stopped in front of a large university building and I wondered if I had the right entrance. I was relieved to see the organizing professor suddenly appear in the doorway and come out to greet me.

"Perfect timing," he said, opening the door for me.

I stepped inside, and there was René standing at the bottom of the college steps.

I was just as surprised to see him as he was to see me. We hadn't seen each other for a while – not since the Safe Justice Encounter had been rejected.

Seeing our surprise, the professor explained, "I thought I would invite the two of you to my class on Restorative Justice. Together you make for a dynamic presentation."

I couldn't help but smile. In the end we had indeed become the dog and pony show – and it had served us well.

Without further explanation, the professor led us down the long hallway and into the classroom where the students were already seated.

René had no problem telling them his story. But when I started to tell my storied *Fifteen Elements*, I was interrupted by one student wanting to tell her victim story – and then another – and another. I glanced at the professor; he didn't intervene but was listening to them intently – almost as if he wanted their stories more than mine.

Not that it mattered to me. If it was a discussion they wanted – we were there to facilitate it. After the class, we debriefed quickly with the professor – but even that was scattered.

I couldn't help but feel that it had been a waste of time and money to bring us halfway across the country when they could have had that conversation all by themselves. But then again, it wasn't my money – only my time.

The next morning at an unearthly hour, René and I found ourselves at the airport gate on our way home to Winnipeg – waiting again. Traveling always meant waiting – checking cellphones – staring out of the window. We tried to do some catch up but I could tell that René was as unsettled as I was.

He would disappear, pace the corridors – and then come back to check on me.

I was huddled by my bag, watching the planes land and lift off.

Finally, he plopped down opposite me.

We started to debrief it again. He had been bewildered by it all as well. Yet we could shrug it off. We had spoken together enough to know that one could never predict what would happen on these speaking tours. Yet no matter what, our travels and our presentations had given us opportunities to work through our own journeys.

The experience had given us an opportunity to deal with our individual black clouds that could have easily defeated us. It had validated us. It had given us rich opportunities to have the most amazing conversations, explore impossible dreams and visit unbelievable places.

In the end, I had not minded sharing the stage with a notorious criminal. The more opposite we were, the more dramatic the story – which meant we had the audience in our hands, and together we could drive our agendas home. Mine was victim awareness with a subplot of forgiveness and moving on. His was prevention, redemption and hope of change.

But it had been hard on us – this was not easy! The stage demanded vulnerability from both of us, with the possibility of always being upstaged and challenged by the sometimes-pointed questions we entertained at the end of our presentations.

He looked as tired as I felt.

Finally, I asked the question on my heart, "Why are we here? What drives you?"

He looked at me – with a bit of a sluggish smirk. "Guilt."

I was shocked at his answer – surprised that after all his work he would still feel guilty.

"And you?" he asked.

I had to search my motives. Excellent question. I drilled down to the bottom of my heart, and was surprised that I had the same answer.

"Guilt," I said. If truth be told, I still felt responsible for the murder of my daughter. If I had picked her up – none of this would be happening. I had failed as a mother. I had failed her when she was alive, and I had failed her in death. All of my programs, all of my efforts, had failed. I felt I had also failed all the murder victims, secondary victims, collared and shackled.

He nodded.

"Will it ever end?" I asked. "This guilt?"

He shook his head – then smiled. "We are stuck with this."

Perhaps the Legislative Women were right. Maybe this was another opportunity to bring meaning to Candace's death – and to recycle the guilt into good as well.

Unbeknownst to the women, Graham was also gaining new enthusiasm for the House. I introduced them to Graham – and there was no controlling the excitement that followed. With the trial out of the way, he saw the possibility of the missing piece in the ideal Journey to Justice program becoming a reality. He was already researching the next steps to develop "the house."

Graham now wanted to know exactly what this house would look like. He believed that our lived experience in the courtroom would give new insights for the dream. It did.

However, there was a bigger issue at hand. I was worried that the victim community as a whole would not endorse the house. He understood this.

There was a group of crime victims who preferred advocacy work. These were the ones who had been directly involved with the movement of victim services from the police department to the courtroom. They were the ones who endorsed the victim impact statement – were vocal – more political, often used by politicians. They were the provincially recognized program, Manitoba Organization of Victim Advocates (MOVA).

I too had worked with MOVA – as a founding member. However, soon after being organized, they began to claim expenses that I couldn't validate. I was working at MCC and could not condone anything that was not accurate. Actually, at this time, I was hearing that most of the grassroots victim organizations across the country were struggling with the same financial irresponsibility. I was puzzled – until I talked to a few of the organizers and realized that for struggling, traumatized victims, the temptations were just too great.

Again, it was another validation that parents of murdered children and others involved with the justice system are stigmatized, which results in them losing their social and financial equity. This is when I decided that, for the Candace House to become a viable proposition, the board structure would have to be professional – and accountable.

We needed something bigger than ourselves.

The problem was that ideally we, as victim organizations, should have been able to coordinate both programs – emotional support and advocacy. We should have been able to work together – but we couldn't.

Graham had worked with MOVA and also with my program, Victims' Voice, so he was well aware of the tension and the big divide.

He was also aware that my forgiveness stance was a constant problem in the victim community.

That's why we needed Candace – a memory bigger than all of us. Candace as a person, and now as a memory, was known for her love for people. She would have to span the philosophical difference because it needed to be safe for both camps – the advocacy group and the support groups.

But how could we ensure buy-in?

Then Graham came up with the brilliant idea to hold a consultation and roll out the idea politically and publicly to all the victim organizations – equally, at the same time.

He started to play with the words. He began the branding process that would be critical in selling the idea of a house to the public.

He used the Legislative Women as a focus group.

"What comes to mind when a person thinks of Candace House?" he asked.

"The Victim comes to the House for Help. The House provides Hope, Help, Hospitality, and Healing while Honoring those that come. 'H' is easy to work with (design-wise) and also forms part of the name Candace House."

Brilliant!

So, it was a process.

But Graham was thinking of more than just a logo.

He continued. "What comes to mind when a person thinks of Candace House?"

As in, "What comes to mind when you hear McDonald's or Tim Hortons? You have an expectation of what you will see and receive if you are there. Each organization has developed an image that they want to promote."

He was teaching us all about branding.

Everyone became involved – even my children. When we needed a logo for the fundraising, I had my two children come up with a logo design – which has remained – with some modification.

The invitation went out – a Candace House Consultation – "Creating a continuum of Care: Closing the gaps by establishing a safe and comforting oasis for Crime Victims" to be held at 61 Carlton Street on January 16, 2014.

It was going to be held at the Dalnavert Museum and Visitors' Centre – a gorgeous old house – two blocks away from the Law Courts Building with ample parking. The house had a modern, public visitor center that wrapped its arms around the house….

Graham had no fear – I was terrified.

It came together beautifully.

The afternoon began with greetings from the Senior Manitoba Federal Cabinet Minister, Shelly Glover, MP, and Manitoba Justice Minister, Andrew Swan, followed by the keynote speech given by the Ombudsman for Victims of Crime, Sue O'Sullivan, who had flown in from Ottawa just to attend.

The room was filled with representatives from every victim organization in the province.

I presented the "Dream of Candace House."

I don't remember much of what I said. I just remember stressing that this would be a building open for all of them to come and do their work. We weren't setting up a competing program; we were simply offering a place to meet and stay. Our first priority was to be a safe place for anyone attending the trial – and this is where my story, my insights, were important.

Graham had the promo materials for them. He addressed the victim workers.

He assured them that this house would be there for Victim Services, Police, Courts, Correctional Service Canada. They could all set up meetings at the house. It would be for professionals – lawyers, psychologists, criminologists. It would be educational with a library, workshops, seminars, and trainings. It would be an opportunity for research and pilot projects, inviting students, and connecting with universities. For crime victims, it would provide programs with themes: rehabilitation, lifestyle, mental health, spiritual, social re-integration and justice.

The guests were then invited to add their vision to ours.

The words we heard were: healing, stress-relieving, warm, comfortable, supportive, non-judgmental, compassionate, loving.

The atmosphere and the roundtable discussions were wonderful.

As far as we could tell, there was a complete buy-in. We taped it all.

We had just given the board the confidence they needed that the vision was sound.

Graham worked swiftly. After the Consultation, he presented a beautiful pamphlet to the board with Dalnavert Museum and Visitors' Centre as a possible house for Candace House.

I was shocked.

Having spent the afternoon there – I could see the potential.

Graham had discovered that this house, which had served as a museum for forty years, had closed the previous fall after the Historical Society found it could no longer afford to operate and maintain it.

He insisted that the Dalnavert Museum was a perfect fit for Candace House, both in terms of its location (on Carlton Street south of Broadway, just a few blocks from the Law Courts) and its warm, welcoming Victorian sensibilities.

To be honest, it was the modern, educational wing that made it viable for us. It would be perfect for group support meetings, press conferences, information and training evenings, fundraising dinners and receptions.

But the adjacent house was also valuable. I particularly loved the dry, spacious basement that could be the perfect, secluded retreat for the grieving family. It was big enough for a day suite.

The upstairs with its small rooms could serve as offices – and the main floor could be a beautiful tea room. We would keep much of the décor.

We would just modernize the kitchen, and set up a few tables in the main floor rooms. The historical significance and the elegance of the décor would be a huge draw….

Many thought that the house might attract the same kind of negative attention from stalking offenders as did shelters for abused women. Would a place of gathering make victims an easy target for anyone disgruntled with the system?

The possibility of a tea room would be perfect – creating the safety of a public place.

Meanwhile, as I was indulging in the dreams, our own case was rolling through the appeal application system. On March 20, 2014, the Supreme Court of Canada accepted the application. I hardly noticed our own crisis in light of the promise of Candace House. The appeal was hardly an issue when something as wonderful as a Candace House was being birthed.

After a critical meeting with the Manitoba Historical Society, it was agreed to transfer Dalnavert Museum and Visitors' Centre to Candace House Inc., a non-profit support center for victims of crime. The Historical Society's office would remain in the house, and a board member would be appointed to the Candace House board, to ensure that we continued to honor the desire of the community in sustaining this historic property.

We felt overwhelming appreciation. We were being saviors of the house – and we were all about being saviors. In turn we would save the victim community.

I'll never forget the day of the announcement. Graham had very discreetly planned to be away on a well-deserved summer holiday. He and his wife had a house on wheels that needed to be used again. They would be gone – and unreachable.

We announced it to the media on April 7, 2014.

The *Winnipeg Free Press* published a very supportive front-page article by Dan Lett. I was photographed in front of the house.

Manitoba Historical Society has agreed to transfer Dalnavert Museum to Candace House Inc., a non-profit support center for the victims of crime.

James Kostuchuk, chairman of the society, said after many months of deliberation, it was decided a partnership with Candace House was the best chance to save the elaborate Victorian mansion.

"With a building like this, you have to be a bit creative," said Kostuchuk. "This is a very good model for other groups about new ways to save important heritage buildings. Our plan is to keep the museum's stories and history alive."

"There is no firm timetable for the opening of Candace House," Derksen said.

Kostuchuk said although the property's title may ultimately transfer to Candace House, MHS will take possession of the property again if the victims' support facility cannot make a go of it.

And even after it has been repurposed, the society will continue to have a presence in the mansion and will retain ownership of all of the possessions in the home.

Another article explained it as well.

The 119-year-old mansion – the former home of Hugh MacDonald, son of prime minister John A. MacDonald – served as a museum for 40 years. It closed last fall after the historical society found it could no longer afford to operate and maintain it.

That's when the society was approached by Wilma Derksen, a noted victims' rights advocate, about repurposing the mansion as a support and education center.

Last year, she revealed a plan to establish Candace House on property near the downtown Law Courts buildings where victims of crime and their families could receive respite, support, and education about the justice system.

Dalnavert Museum is a perfect fit for Candace House, both in terms of its location (on Carlton Street south of Broadway, just a few blocks from the Law Courts) and its warm, welcoming Victorian sensibilities.

There is no firm timetable for the opening of Candace House, Derksen said.

And even after it has been repurposed, the society will continue to have a presence in the mansion and will retain ownership of all of the possessions in the home.

And then the roof caved in.

Overnight. On April 24, 2014. One week later. We heard via social media that we had opposition. A reporter called me.

The next day there was another article in the newspaper.

Winnipeg heritage group is holding out hope that the Dalnavert Museum building can still be a museum, rather than be converted into a drop-in center for victims of crime.

Cindy Tugwell of Heritage Winnipeg says she was surprised to learn of plans to turn the historic mansion into Candace House, the brainchild of victims' rights advocate Wilma Derksen.

Tugwell said she wants Dalnavert to be kept as a museum, with some upgrades.

"Give us an opportunity to see if this museum can be sustainable," she told CBC News on Thursday.

"It can reinvent itself; it can be a museum of the 21st century, and I know there's other historic home museums across the country we can use as models."

Tugwell said Heritage Winnipeg had submitted a proposal in January to save the museum, only to learn in a newspaper story that its bid wasn't accepted and Derksen's was.

Derksen has said Candace House won't be a home for victims of crime, but it will be similar to a drop-in center, staffed with counsellors and support workers.

"We don't really know the requirements right now of Candace House from a physical standpoint of what kind of space they need, what kind of requirements," Tugwell said. "So, we'd love to sit down with Mrs. Derksen and if that's a possibility, it certainly would be on the table."

I set up a meeting....

But in the meantime – I went to a large social event in our area and had a chance to talk to some long-standing Winnipeg people with an interest in history. They were upset with me. I was violating the history of the city. I saw it through their eyes.

They changed my mind about it all.

I was all about history. In fact, I had a tiny museum in our own house, similar to what my father had before me. I respected history.

I could see the conflict – unnecessary really.

If the house was symbolic of the past, the Candace House did not belong in it.

I believe that people with a forgiveness orientation tend to be future-oriented. Just as those in a positive mindset tend to be future-oriented – and those with negative mindsets often tend to be fixated on the past.

Candace House needed to be about imagining new beginnings.

Candace House needed to be about forgiveness – moving into the future – a forward motion.

Yet – Graham was nowhere to be reached. I tried but it was impossible to connect with him. We assumed he was traveling, exploring somewhere off-grid. There was only a tiny window of opportunity – we could not wait.

We, as the executive committee of Candace House, had an emergency meeting and decided that we needed to withdraw immediately. We notified the other board members, and we all agreed.

I called the reporter.

And the next day there was another article.

Wilma Derksen has abandoned her plan to turn the former Dalnavert Museum into Candace House, a sanctuary for victims of crime and their families.

Derksen said on Friday that she didn't realize the plan would stir up contention with heritage groups, even though the Manitoba Historical Society agreed to the plan.

"We just didn't realize the controversy or the protection of the house that was still there. We thought that it was negotiable and that people were open to a new plan, a new re-purposing of Dalnavert," she said.

"We want to respect other people's opinions and for them to work it out."

Heritage Winnipeg said it had submitted a proposal in January to save the museum and was shocked to find out through the media that its bid wasn't accepted, and instead, the building would become a center for victims.

"I do have to admit, we are very disappointed. It seemed to be so perfect," Derksen said, adding she will continue looking for another location to open Candace House.

It was over.

I had failed Candace again.

An enormous reptilian cloud was on the move, circling – sucking the energy out of me. I was so tired of it all.

When Graham came back – the dream house was gone. He was devastated.

He maintained that, if all interested parties had had an opportunity to meet, we could have reached a compromise. The property was large enough that we could have created space in the Visitors' Centre or main building for everyone. His guess was that most members of the heritage community were not aware that we had agreed to add a Historical Society member to our board and to provide continued office space for them in Dalnavert. He didn't see any of the expressed concerns as insurmountable.

Graham was right. He probably could have done it....

It was hard to listen to him – knowing that he could have done it. But the will wasn't there anymore. It wasn't in the board; it wasn't in the community, and it wasn't in me.

I doubted if he would ever forgive me.

I'm not sure anyone would forgive me for acting so arbitrarily.

As always, there is a lot of blame at times like this, and I started to hear rumblings that the board had lost confidence in me as well as in Graham. There had been too many tiny bits of miscommunication. No one felt comfortable anymore.

I really thought the dream of the house would die at that point! It was gone. I was done.

Many friends, and even some extended family, told me that I should let it die. The tide had turned. No one could recover from something like this. Boards can only take so much – and the city of Winnipeg wouldn't react kindly to such a hostile public debate.

Graham resigned.

The president of the board resigned.

When I realized that the board had lost confidence in me as well, I was tempted to resign.

It was all going to die.... All that learning was going to be lost.

But before I could walk away, I needed to try one more thing. Perhaps the vision needed new people, new blood.

New blood, new people – new vision?

I remembered a young student, Cecilly Hildebrand, whom I had hired for a summer job program to organize a roundtable discussion designed to unpack the troublesome concept of forgiveness and discuss how it affects our lives after murder. It was in preparation for the Safe Justice Program. I really wanted to find a new way of dealing with the controversial "forgiveness" word by replacing it with the word "resilience."

We called it the "Unpacking the 'F-Word' Consultation." We invited high-profile murder victims from across the country for a one-day dialogue.

We had hired three amazing speakers who had all claimed the forgiveness word – and lived it.

We began the roundtable with one of the speakers telling us his transformational story of wanting the woman who killed his mother to hang and then fighting for the abolition of the death penalty. He was so perfect for long discussions on resilience. I had just decided that it was possible to talk about the transformation and healing without the word when Bill stood up at the end and said, "You know…. I can't help but believe – as I'm watching all of you – that there is one thing missing in our conversation."

Everyone waited – he was right. The conversations had been good in and of themselves – but, even though they had all talked about healing and transformation, there hadn't been the force and power of it….

Then he said, "You have to forgive…." There was the "f" word again.

Then he added, "You have to forgive yourself!"

Later, all the participants said that it had been the most healing time together. They thanked me profusely – and ended with, "Bill is right – we have to forgive ourselves."

Oh yuk! There was that word again! Forgiveness!

I had set up the entire conference to look for a different word – and yet at the end – the entire group jelled on that word. We had chosen forgiveness over resilience. It was inescapable.

But there was also something else that had happened. A few of this group had asked me, "We really like Cecilly. Could we invite her to group?" This was the group that said that no one understood a murder victim except another murder victim.

I took note. Cecilly had no experience of murder.

And that's why, when everything was falling apart, I thought of Cecilly. It had been years since I had seen her.

I simply asked her in an email, "Are you bored?" When she answered me with curiosity, we set up a meeting. She had all kinds of other grand plans – but she did take on the job.

We eventually hired her as Executive Director of Candace House.

The other person I selected was the owner of the IBEX Payroll Company, Darryl Stewart. I had met him when he asked me to speak to the Winnipeg Executive Association, made up of successful local businesses, on their annual inspiration day. We had met for coffee previously at Starbucks on Corydon – and I was impressed with his charm, his thoroughness – and his curiosity around forgiveness and how it applied to the business culture. It was while we were having coffee that I started to wonder if this was the man. Then, at the actual meeting, I watched him closely. I liked the way he moved so easily through the crowd. They respected him – talked to him – praised him. He seemed oblivious of his role – and his casual leadership style.

There was something about him that reminded me of Candace's charisma.

I asked him if he needed another challenge. He had no idea what I had in mind for him.

He was a true businessman, and this house was a business – similar to a rental. The house would be filled with tenants.

Graham and I were too program oriented. We loved collecting people to gather, to have dialogues – it had worked in the past. But this wasn't about the program – at least it wouldn't be for a while – perhaps a long while.

We had to trust the DNA that was in the proposal for Candace House.

I knew that it was on a good foundation – one that Graham had articulated so brilliantly – so I could let it sail.

And it was working. The board meetings were even being held in a new place.

I had left my house early to attend our third board meeting – anxious, as always, whether this new set of people could and would work together. A quarter of the way there, I felt really ill and turned into a fast-food restaurant for a pit stop. I think I had to stop three times. This wasn't a flu, headache, cold, or fever. It felt like food poisoning or something like that.

After the third stop, I remember getting into my car – bracing myself as I was driving – determined to get to this meeting. I was going to be there because they needed me.

But I was so sick – and, by this time, weak. The reptilian cloud had sucked out too much. I didn't have any energy.

I didn't want to let anyone down.

I thought of both René and Graham who were still part of it – whether they knew it or not. René had planted the seed when he started the fund in prison and then continued to raise money by giving everything he earned speaking to schools as a donation to the Candace Derksen Fund with The Winnipeg Foundation.

And at one point, when we discussed the creation of a Safe Justice House, he had said, "The name is no good. Let's call it Candace House." I was not pleased. I knew it was a ploy on their part to keep me involved as a token victim. I wanted to say, "No. Let's keep Candace out of it."

Graham, with his skill in writing proposals and his passion for helping those who were marginalized and in trouble with the law – victim or offender – had moved us to a point where we had a visual image and a concrete example of how to do it. He had a way of making our harebrained ideas respectable.

The breakfasts, especially the breakfast with Alan Libman, the victim-offender encounters, the conversations, the meetings, the daring, the weeping, the joys, the sorrows, the writing – and the constant struggle to understand the world we lived in – had all led us to this point.

It had been a long, arduous journey – the crisscrossing of the country – the writing – the effort – the tedious search to find the perfect word in my writings.

It had taken us a long time to come up with a very simple idea.

But there was no denying – I was sick and tired.

And yet I was driven – guilt!

Then all of a sudden, I felt something shift. It was almost a Damascus experience. Candace was in the car.

"Mom, I've got this," she said, with her winning smile.

I fought the tears – and kept on driving. Clearly, I was tired and going out of my mind.

Then I tested it – whatever it was in the car with me. "Candace, do you really have this?"

"Yes, Mom."

Really – of course – it had always been about Candace. She had guided this whole trip, and now she wanted to take the wheel. The presence left. I had arrived at some truth.

"Then take it away, Candace!!!!"

And I turned the car around and never went back to another board meeting – except to visit. Clearly, they could do this without my help. They didn't know it, but Candace was in charge.

Candace was all about love – and forgiveness.

Candace was our sanguine child. She was the one who had inherited a strong love for people.

I recall how, even as a four-year-old, when we had moved into a new community, she had gone out on the front steps and banged on pots and pans. When I asked her what she was doing, she had told me to wait. There was mischief in her eyes. And then, exactly as she planned, all the little children came out of their houses to see what the racket was about.

Her love for people, translated into this situation now, would mean that she would be very worried about the safety of other children. She would want truth. She would want her story told so that the community would be armed against all sexual predators.

On the other hand, she also loved the bullies in the class. An elementary teacher had told us that Candace was so gifted in dealing with bullies that she had often assigned her to them – even at that young age.

Candace would also have wanted to hold onto the hope that the accused would confess, change – and, by being healed, become safe enough to enter society again.

She simply loved people. As I struggle with all my inner questions, I am grateful that I can still feel her presence – I can still feel that love that has carried us all this time. In the first book that I wrote, I chose "love" as the last word to end it.

She was the one who embodied the spirit of the house.

The car was filled with light – her presence in the car had removed the clouds.

Now I could step back and breathe life into my daughter's memory and let them take it away.

Cecilly, Darryl and the new board members had the youth, the naivete, the idealism, the skill, the already-drafted and written proposals to truly make it happen.

I drove home and resigned from the board shortly after.

That same fall on September 17, 2014, I flew to Royal Roads University on Vancouver Island to take a course in Executive Coaching.

Shortly after, Graham and his wife embarked on their lifetime dream to retire and visit forty-eight states and ten provinces in their motor home.

René was vacationing with his extended family in Florida.

Alan Libman remained on the board as our family's representative.

It took the new board four years to rebuild our shattered dream of Dalnavert to make the House their own. And it was not an easy time for them. I think they went through the same process all over again – and came up with the same conclusions we had. It was necessary! The dream of a Candace House was worth fighting for.

I always felt a little guilty – but tried not to interfere.

Candace House opened on November 26, 2018 (almost thirty-four years to the day that Candace went missing.)

The headlines read:

"It's beauty. It's sorrow": Newly opened Candace House helps families of victims heal

Families who lost a loved one to homicide now have a safe place of comfort during trials....

Candace House is the culmination of Derksen's vision for a safe haven for victims and their families navigating their way through the criminal justice system.

One or two families at a time will have daytime access to the home, full of warm colors and soft couches, to relax before and after visiting the Law Courts a block away.

"When we experience true beauty, it brings out the tears in us. It's beauty. It's sorrow. It's remembering all of the grief we went through," said Derksen, pointing out a soundproof ceiling in the house where families can cry and grieve.

The home-like atmosphere includes a living room, dining room, kitchen, play area for children, and a special space for sacred smudging.

Art adorns the walls of the Kennedy Street space. In the corner, a sculpture of Candace, created by her father Cliff, sits on a top bookshelf. It depicts Candace's arms that were bound when she was murdered, showing them now free. And in the middle, a locket she was wearing when her body was found.

...And in the few short weeks Candace House has been open, it has already been doing that. The family of 18-year-old Nicholas Brophy spent days there as they awaited the verdict in their son's murder trial.

A picture of Brophy sits on a table near the entrance. Executive director Cecilly Hildebrand read out a thank-you letter from his family at the grand opening.

"Candace House will always be part of the Brophy family. We will never forget your kindness. Your willingness to help us every step of the way. With much gratitude, the Brophy family," it says.

Executive director Cecilly Hildebrand says Candace House is the first of its kind and is already looking to expand to offer counseling, programs and possibly space for a community support group.

More than half of the $280,000 in renovations that transformed the commercial space into Candace House has come from private donations. More than $50,000 is from the province's department of victim services. Families who lost a loved one to homicide now have a safe place of comfort during trials.

On the day of the opening, I knew that the new board members deserved every bit of praise they were getting. It was their house.

Yet, in reality, many made it happen. Too many to name – and I was thankful for each one of them.

And then there was Candace.

Cliff and I have often said that our main contribution to this world is our children. We've had three. None of them were planned; they all came at the most awkward times for us. But each had a very important reason to be here.

Candace was the first. Then there is Odia, our second who is flourishing in Southern Manitoba working for Friesens Corporation as the Corporate Marketing Manager. She and Larry have Georgia, their long-awaited child. Larry is pastoring. They have a lovely house in Winkler. She's a talented artist like her father – and has an amazing leadership presence. Syras, our third, has a lovely house in Lindenwoods and is flourishing as a psychologist – with his own private practice and an established clinic on Pembina Highway. Together with his wife, he is now pastor of Maplecrest Church. Natasha is homeschooling their two children, Simeon and Anna.

Since Syras is featured regularly on radio, he is sought out for his psychological wisdom and has become well known in Winnipeg.

Odia and Syras are so talented. The world will continue to notice them on their own, so I'm going to let them find their way.

And now I could also let Candace find her own way.

I'm going to describe Candace, who is no longer with us but still is.

Even as a toddler, she would just shine when we were with others. She loved people and had a wit way beyond her years. She made extraordinary connections with everyone.

And I'm not just saying that in hindsight. I distinctly remember a time when a friend and I were watching our two little girls playing.

My friend, who was a bit disappointed in her child, said, "I'm reading an article in the *Reader's Digest* – and I'm so tired of parents who write, in such glowing terms, about their children who have died – no one is that good. I could never write that kind of article about mine."

And I looked outside, watching Candace – her hair floating in the breeze – her giggle ringing through the air. I didn't say anything. I wanted to respect the pain of my friend, but I remember thinking, "I could write that about Candace." Candace was a pure spirit of light and love. She wasn't perfect, but even in her raw moments, she had an indescribably beautiful spirit. My second thought was, "I hope I never have to write that article." Ironically – I did. Decades later *Reader's Digest* published an article on Candace.

I could go on and on.

It all came to a head when Candace started to become a woman. As a teen, her love for her friends became even more noticeable.

She adopted a theme song, "Friends are Friends Forever," which she played every night before she went to sleep. The song's words haunt me.

In the Father's hands, we know
That a lifetime's not too long to live as friends

227

Before moving to Winnipeg, we had lived in North Battleford, Saskatchewan for almost five years, and Candace had developed a very special relationship with a friend, who lived across the street, two houses down. The two had been inseparable.

When we moved to Manitoba, it was heartbreaking to watch Candace mourn her best friend. As a going-away present, Tracy had bought Candace a gold-toned locket. Candace treasured that locket and wore it all the time. Even after it began to tarnish, she still wore it.

This worried me a little. I wondered if she was making the necessary adjustment to our move, or if, for some reason, she still needed Tracy emotionally. I thought that when she met Heidi at Camp Arnes, and they started to become good friends, the necklace would come off, but it hadn't.

One time, when we were traveling through Saskatoon, we made a special effort to revisit North Battleford so that Candace could see Tracy. I thought that if everything had gone as life usually does, the two girls — now almost young women — would have changed so much that the bond wouldn't be as strong. The memories would be replaced, and Candace would put the necklace away.

I was secretly a little happy when we arrived at her house to find that Tracy had another friend visiting her. Just as I suspected, Tracy had changed. I felt a little sorry for Candace as I watched the two girls, once so close, now stand awkwardly apart, assessing each other. We spent the afternoon with them, and by the time we left, the girls were enjoying themselves. Still, there was a noticeable distance between them. The good-byes were warm, but not tearful.

Driving back, I gently prodded her.

"Tracy has changed?"

"Yes."

"You've changed?"

"Yes."

"It's not quite the same?"

Cliff gave me a warning look telling me that I should leave the girl alone, but the question was already in the air.

Her voice was quiet but steady. "No, it wasn't the same."

I glanced back. She was looking out the window, fingering her necklace as she said, "It doesn't matter how much we change." She turned to look at me. "At the end of the visit, I saw the old Tracy. She'll always be my friend."

She was wearing that necklace the day she disappeared.

The police brought it to us....

Years later, I received this letter....

First, I would just like to say a few things about Candace and what she meant to me.

Candace imprinted on my soul. ...I was one of many kids who she engaged, on her own initiative, to lead, to play with, to pay attention to and love. When you are a younger girl, winning the attention of an older girl is akin to winning the lottery. There is no greater achievement at that stage of life. Candace accepted this misfit with ease, integrity and without any positioning or arrogance. It was natural to her and she seemed indifferent to our differences.

As an adopted, mixed race kid in the late 70s and 80s, who was racially discriminated against, sometimes violently, moved to different several schools in various countries, with an accent; everything I did was about trying to fit in. The weekend we went to camp, the trepidation I had dissipated the instant I was introduced to Candace. Her genuine acceptance of me without a second thought was so off putting that I think I didn't speak for hours. I just followed her around in wonder. Plus, she had the inside track at camp which involved access to the tuck shop.

Ever after that weekend, she was famous to me...even then....

People were falling in love with her – even after she was gone. Some said that she had powers. When things were particularly difficult at Child Find Manitoba, they had said they were inspired, encouraged by something almost otherworldly. They had felt the presence of Candace that led them through the darkness. They called her pixie dust – a magical effect that brings great success or luck.

Now there was a Candace House, and I wasn't entirely surprised. People need love.

Victims need a safe place where they are treated like they are number one! A place in the justice system where their needs are first, offenders second.

The House is really about her love – that amazing power of love – a love that outshines justice – and that keeps the clouds at bay.

It looks a little like pixie dust.

Chapter 22
SOCIAL EXPERIMENT

I really thought it was over, that I had dealt with it all – and then I received this startling email from Johann Hari.

...I am writing to request an interview with you for a book I am writing supporting the Circles of Support and Accountability program, where I admire your advocacy more than I can say.

I am a British journalist who has written for the New York Times, the Guardian, the Los Angeles Times, Le Monde and others. I have written two New York Times best-selling books – one about the drug war, and the other about depression – which have been praised by a broad range of people, from Noam Chomsky to Hillary Clinton to Richard Dawkins. My TED talk has been viewed over 25 million times....

I will be in Toronto from the 12th April to early on the 16th. I am writing a book that assesses the Circles program and your story is so important.

It was dated March 25, 2019.

Circles of Support and Accountability?

How did a famous writer living in England know about it? Few people knew about my connection with Circles of Support and Accountability – better known as CoSA.

But he was right! Of all the programs I had encountered in the Criminal Justice System, I did support this unusual community-based program. I thought it was brilliant.

As victims we have three basic needs. We want a sense of justice that will prevent what happened to us from ever happening again.

We don't want anyone else to have to endure what we have had to live through. We want the person annihilated or under some kind of control.

The second need is validation. It isn't only the crime that has devastated us – it is the stigmatization of the crime as well. We want vindication so that we can enter back into society.

Thirdly, we need to know what happened and why so we can turn our victimization into a learning experience and hopefully create some meaning out of it.

CoSA promised prevention – not only a quick fix but a long-term prevention through accountability, connection and rehabilitation. It was the most daring program I had encountered.

I was introduced to the program when I was asked to do a training for them shortly after they became established.

After telling my story and listing the *Fifteen Elements*, I listened to their stories. The room was full of ordinary community members who were fiercely dedicated to working with high-risk sex offenders that had been released to the community. They were passionate about their "core member" – the ex-inmate – and attending to his needs – holding him accountable by being his friend and watchdog – acting like a group sponsor.

They were versed in all the manipulative games of inmates, knew all the triggers and excuses, yet were willing to engage in restoration, reintegration, and risk management of the offenders.

At that time the program had been around for only about ten years – a movement that was started by Mennonite Pastor Harry Nigh, who befriended a sex offender and believed that, by forming a connection and developing a circle of support and accountability, he could keep the community safe. He had developed a simple formula – meeting with the core member once a week and staying in touch with him every day via an old-fashioned pager.

Soon after the training, I was asked to speak at an Ontario CoSA conference in Waterloo. It was part of a larger speaking tour covering

Toronto and the surrounding area. For this one, I needed to get to Waterloo.

My chauffeur was Eileen Henderson, manager of the Circles Initiative in the Toronto, Hamilton and Kitchener area.

The trip promised to be uneventful. I found her easy to talk to. She was gracious, forthright and affirming as she asked about my life. It was easy to process with her. The Mazda van was spacious and comfortable.

And then she received a call on her cellphone and answered it – which at the time wasn't illegal.

It was a call from the Toronto Police informing her that a high-risk sex offender had just been seen talking to a child, violating his parole order, and had been taken into custody.

Visibly shaken, Eileen flew into action – handling it all. This was her responsibility.

She never missed a beat. She cooperated with the police without hesitation. "Glad you took him in…."

Then she was on the phone to the probation officer finding out the details of the offense and then connecting with all of her staff to let them know of the breach of his agreement with CoSA.

Violation, breach, child at risk. The air was tense.

We were driving down the 401 – one of North America's busiest highway, carrying almost half a million people per day – passing through Toronto. Near Pearson International Airport the road is eighteen lanes wide.

She was on the phone. She was a good driver – but now distracted. The car was sometimes hovering on the edge of the highway then speeding up to pass the occasional car that was even slower than us – and then another and another – and then back to a snail's pace. I wasn't sure which was more dangerous – slow or fast – on this crowded highway.

But she was a petite superwoman negotiating it. Talking down the distressed community member who was on supervisory duty, telling them that they no longer had access to him because his pager had been confiscated but that they might want to attend the bail hearing the next day to be supportive. Then talking to the prison chaplain, asking him to go and see the offender now in custody.

Through it all, it was clear that she not once condoned or defended the core member but was very clear on the desired outcome – to not lose connection, to not abandon him even if he had breached.

"We are not dumping him," she said.

After it was settled and the car was under control again, I was full of questions.

She described it simply. Sex offenders being released into the community were given a chance to join the program if their goal was to not reoffend.

Most core members were motivated by prevention. "No more victims." But some core members were motivated by not wanting to go back to jail. "I'm too old to do that again."

She was not a con-lover but definitely a support person who knew the importance of holding someone accountable – with love and firmness.

Why did she do this?

She didn't need the money. Her husband's position as CEO of a large equipment company gave her the freedom to work in these demanding non-profit positions that paid very little. Helping others was her life. Her soul. Actually, she was doing what she and her husband both found fascinating and fulfilling.

Somehow, we got to Waterloo – and I could tell my story to these CoSA heroes with new admiration.

After that, Eileen and I stayed in touch – and observing her work and the program for over seventeen years – I became a true believer in the program.

On the day of the acquittal of the man accused of murdering our daughter, I saw three chaplains in the courtroom. Since the accused had already been designated as a high-risk sex offender, I knew he would qualify for a CoSA program – if not formally at least informally. Those chaplains were committed to supporting him.

My need for prevention had been satisfied. I was quite verbal in my blogs at that time about my belief in CoSA.

So I wasn't surprised when, right after the verdict of acquittal, the organizers of the Ottawa CoSA chapter asked me to speak at their annual fundraising gala.

It had been a significant trip for me on many levels.

While in Ottawa, the organizer set me up with two other appointments.

I was to meet a man I didn't know at the Grill 41 Restaurant and Bar, a stone's throw away from the Rideau Canal, Confederation Park and Parliament Hill. Apparently, this man had a story I had to hear. He was a core member of CoSA.

He was sitting by the window when I arrived, already with a cup of coffee – a sweet, kind-looking man. Bookish, I thought, as I slid into the booth.

We were both nervous – being forced to talk to each other this way.

We talked about the ice storm that had moved through the city earlier that week. We talked about the organizer, the arranger of this meeting, as we both ordered muffins – banana and carrot.

Then I started asking questions – it seems to be my role in life.

"When did it happen?"

"Early eighties," he said.

Then we paused.

"This feels as if I am meeting the mother of my victim – the offenses are similar," he said carefully.

With just a few questions, I realized that he had been following all my blogs, my books, starting with my very first book about Candace.

He had spent thirty-six years in prison. "I was in deep denial for the first seventeen," he explained.

There were some sexual assaults before the murder of a sixteen-year-old girl. After a small party, she had left with him and then rejected his advances. He strangled her.

"My life had no value so I didn't think anyone's life had value. I felt I deserved it. I felt entitled. She was denying me something that was mine."

He was open about his mental health treatment. He had been diagnosed with sexual disorders, sadism and hebephilia. He had been attracted to pubescent and adolescent girls.

"I process things differently – always have ever since age six."

After hearing his story – I felt that I too was meeting with the person who had killed our daughter. I had met many convicted, guilty criminals who had told me their stories. Some had done horrendous crimes – but this time I felt the similarity. He fit the profile of someone who could have taken Candace.

I felt a chill run through me.

He continued his story.

When he first got out of jail, his social anxiety was acute. "I was scared to get on a bus full of people. I couldn't even walk down the middle of a sidewalk. I was always on the edge."

He has been on day parole for two years and has already served one year. He was in the CoSA program. "I don't want to kill anyone ever – I don't want to go back to prison. I am motivated."

It was hard to imagine him wanting to kill anyone – he seemed so timid, gentle and frail.

"I can't ever forget maintenance – the weekly meetings. I am building the person I want to be – I like the person I am today."

He has had a great deal of psychological help – starting with a twelve-session Victim Impact Program that consisted of three parts: accountability, study of ten different crimes, and forgiveness.

He said he has read my book, *Confronting the Horror* – which was worn and tattered with use.

I asked him what the hardest step in his choice to change had been. He said it was moving through his denial.

"Denial doesn't keep the community safe," he said. "Prevention comes with healing."

236

Then he lingered on forgiveness. He needed to forgive his upbringing, himself, and the victims who will not forgive him. He had worked hard to change himself. He said that he had fought hard against being held hostage by their anger.

I could hear the truth in his words – the remorse – the sadness. I felt compassion.

For years I had wondered what it would be like to meet the man who had killed our daughter – wondering if I might be overcome with the intensity of those tumultuous clouds. Would I be left forever bitter?

At one point, I thought it might be possible to meet him when the police charged him with first degree murder. But then, because of legal restrictions, I couldn't access the man who was accused – and after his acquittal there was no point. I had to accept the fact that there would never be a "meeting" – something that symbolized a satisfactory closure for me.

Now, here I was sitting with a person fitting the profile of the man who had killed my daughter – and I didn't feel that same repulsion.

Both of us realized together that there is no such thing as satisfactory justice for either of us. No closure – and no hope of closure.

Some actions cannot be undone.

Yet something had changed in the Grill 41 Restaurant and Bar.

Years ago, I had been repulsed and upset with a notorious criminal speaking to a gymnasium of high school students.

And now, here I was sitting with a man who fit the profile of everything I hated – and I felt compassion. In fact, I was not resenting him but learning from him.

I was learning once again that, in the end, forgiveness isn't about reconciliation.

We can't put our healing processes in the control of another person. Reconciliation takes two – and if the other doesn't cooperate or isn't available, we are forever suspended. We have to do it for ourselves. By working on our own issues – forgiving ourselves, pursuing truth, even finding answers through surrogate conversations – we can take back our lives – and find our personal justice satisfaction. Forgiveness is intended to set us free.

All the work that I had done to forgive and make peace with my many clouds had worked.

In some ways it was as if both of us had climbed our personal Mount Everest and now, having conquered it, we could enjoy the view together.

There wasn't a cloud in sight. The sky was a beautiful blue.

Now this amazing email from Johann Hari!

Was that how Johann had heard about me – through the CoSA Ottawa event?

The email continued…. "Would it be possible for me to come to interview you? I would send you anything I quote from you for you to fact-check. I'd be thrilled if this was possible but I know you are really busy so I understand if it's not."

Of course, I would love to meet him! I immediately ordered his book, *Lost Connections, Uncovering the Real Causes of Depression*, which has been translated into twenty-seven languages and has been praised by a broad range of people.

I simply devoured it. I felt it was the missing piece – the academic understanding – what I had learned the hard way. Plus he had the narrative ability to make all of his research readable. And, best of all, he had come to the same conclusion that I had in my own personal journey. It was all about connection.

We set a date. He asked me to arrange a place to meet.

I wondered: Where do you meet someone like Johann Hari? Did he want to meet others perhaps? Should I book a ballroom and invite guests? I was almost beside myself.

I gave him options – an upscale restaurant or a diner with local flavor?

He didn't care. He simply wanted to meet me for lunch and interview me. That was clear. "You choose."

After much deliberation, I chose Aaltos at the Canad Inns on Pembina. It had easy access, great parking, spacious patio-like indoor setting, no blaring music and an unpretentious clientele.

It was the perfect day – rainy, wet and gray – probably as British as Winnipeg weather ever gets.

Johann was a few minutes late. He recognized me immediately and slipped into the booth opposite – as if we were old friends. Casual and friendly.

But there was something about him – something magical.

Each server that came by was mesmerized with him.

I didn't know if it was because they knew he was famous or if he just had that kind of charismatic energy to change the atmosphere around him.

In any case, I was again invisible to the servers as they hovered over him. They didn't hear me or see me. In fact, when it came to ordering, Johann had to order for me.

None of it mattered. I, too, was under the spell of his charm. He handled it all with ease.

Then after the chitchat, he put his recorder near my plate and we talked.

I don't remember what we talked about – except that the word "connection" was used a lot. After reading his book, it seemed it was my word as much as it was his. His stories, research and theories validated so much of what I had experienced.

I just remember reassessing everything while reading his book. In Canada, living in the post-death-penalty era, we couldn't deny that we had evolved to a new place.

So what should this new place look like?

What do we do with people that have murdered? Perhaps the answer is to not disconnect permanently, as we had thought traditionally, and put them behind bars.

We might have to disconnect for a time, but we should do so with the intention of reconnection – because we, as human beings, need connection to stay human.

The hope is that if we do this carefully and responsibly – we will all learn more about each other and ourselves. We will heal together.

Johann listened to me intently – I hoped I was able to contribute to his new book.

In turn, he gave me something beautiful – his story.

Johann tells the story of travelling to Vietnam to research his next book. Once there, beside the hotel in the market, he saw a large, very red and inviting apple which he bought, washed and ate. It proved to be contaminated and he became dangerously ill.

Against his wishes, he was taken to a hospital. After apologizing to the doctor about the "unglamorous aspect" of his explosive nausea, the doctor said, "We need your nausea. It is a message and we must listen to the message. It will tell us what is wrong with you. We need to listen to it."

Johann realized that the nausea – a symptom that he didn't want – that he hated – had actually been a signal that saved his life.

In the same way, the black clouds were a symptom of my fear, anger and grief. Enlarged. I had fought them, hated them. But in hindsight, now I can see that they were also my guides.

They had guided me through those seven, long, dark weeks looking for Candace, then twenty-three years through the mists of mystery till a man was charged. Right into the labyrinth of the trial process – the preliminary that lasted fourteen days, the trial of twenty-five days, through the appeal process, ending in a retrial which lasted another twenty-five days. The entire justice process had taken seventy-two days in all – about three months – spread out over a ten-year time period.

Those clouds, shapeshifting as we went along, had been my constant guide.

After Johann left, I went home to ponder the conversation.

What would this connection look like in my ideal world?

As long as we have offender types reeling out of control, being anti-social and preying on our vulnerable, we will always need prisons. Out of necessity we need to disconnect to keep the victims safe. But we shouldn't use this time to punish but to begin to rebuild. Offenders need support and appropriate ways of processing and healing their story. They need a controlled space.

For the victims affected by homicide, they need to be given space to disconnect as well, as they enter into their healing process. They don't need a controlled space, but a safe place that understands them.

So both need to disconnect for a time, and then both need to find a way to connect back into society.

The offenders might need to resort to symbolic gestures – such as the beading program and "redemption work." They need to replace their irresponsibility with works of responsibility and the system should provide them with opportunities to do that. I learned this from René. They need to show they have changed. They need to earn their redemption and right to connect.

For the victims to reconnect to society and their community, they need to find the right words to describe their journey from darkness to light. They need to conquer their black clouds. Until they move past their hurt – their inclination to vengeance and anger will feel unsafe to the community they wish to reconnect with.

So, in many ways, the paths of offenders and victims are the same.

Then how do we reconnect again? My one regret is that we never did solve the "encounter" problem. How do we make peace between the victims and offenders in murder and other serious crime? How do we help them dispel their dark clouds? How do we help them to reconnect?

As long as we have prisons and a Criminal Justice System that keep victims and offenders legally separate, we have the problem of those uncontrolled intersections where they will meet and continue the harm that they did to each other in the past.

I wonder if perhaps the justice system needs to find a way of controlling the intersection. Perhaps it could be a Post-Crime Reconciliation Registry (PCRR) which would allow victims to post a private victim impact statement, and an offender to post a private apology. If there was a match, the Registry could provide them with the place and time for a safe encounter.

But we can't make the mistake of placing this critical "connection" program in either camp – victim or offender. This PCRR would need to be housed in a neutral place, perhaps with a psychological association, with a clear mandate that both parties would be supported by their own identified, informed and recognized independent support system, such as a Candace House for victims and a John Howard Society for offenders – a place where they are innately understood.

Perhaps this could also be a place for both victim and offenders to post their wish for a surrogate encounter – perhaps not ideal but one that could still be effective for those who choose to embrace the process – as it was for me.

Each encounter I participated in dispelled a cloud or two.

There was another significant event that happened in Ottawa.

After the Grill 41 Restaurant and Bar meeting, I went to my next appointment. This meeting was with a professor from Algonquin College in the Victimology and Police Foundations department, who had a request.

"We would love to create a short film of your story while you are here that can continue to be used as a learning tool for students and survivors. The victimology program will pay for the cost of filming."

By this time, I was preoccupied with my new career, working as a therapist at the Oakville Wellness Centre.

Perhaps if I had someone to share this with?

I answered, almost without thinking. "I would like to include my husband's art."

He just nodded. "And what would that look like?"

Cliff's journey had paralleled mine.

After the preliminary, he had started working in clay in an entirely new way. By this time, he was renting space at the Clifton Studios and took advantage of any break in his business to create art.

The professor was waiting.... I described Cliff, his art, and the chance of a combined exploration of our journey together. He thought it was a great idea.

Once I was home, I frantically went to work scripting the narrative. I was pleasantly surprised to discover that while I was isolating fifteen elements, Cliff had also created fifteen sculptures that, with a bit of creativity, we could make work together. It was amazing, comforting, confirming and, in some ways, astounding to find that we truly had been on the same journey.

Since we didn't have a gallery at our disposal, we decided on a pop-up show, for which we would rent a few white plinths and set up at strategic places around Winnipeg to showcase his art.

In preparation, we spent an entire Sunday exploring our lovely city – appreciating it even more as we remembered how supportive this city had been for us. Cliff and I had to choose a unique setting for each sculpture.

The filming was going to be a whirlwind tour of our sprawling city.

As planned, two young men flew into Winnipeg – cameras on their shoulders.

The first day, at eight o'clock in the morning, in the U-Haul we had rented, we drove north twenty-eight kilometers to Lockport where the floodway joins the Red. Near the river's edge, with the tumbling water in view, we set up the first sculpture, *Werewolf* – steel black, vicious, representing the uncontrollable rage both Cliff and I had experienced.

Then we drove down Henderson Highway to the Nairn overpass, near where we had once lived. It was like driving down memory lane. We had chosen a place under the overpass because we believed the abductor had taken Candace along this route to the shed where her body was found. Cliff remembers checking it out during his own frantic search that first night – screaming for her. Had she heard him? Under the overpass we set up Cliff's *Throne of Swords*, representing the terror and fear that we had both felt. It was by the railway tracks – and a train rolled by as we filmed.

Very close by – with our former home in view – we set up the sculpture that represented complicated grief. *Seven Weeks* captured Cliff's own grief. As an artist, Cliff had wanted to identify with Candace in her excruciating, painful death, and had started sculpting her tied-up hands. But when it came to sculpting her hands, he couldn't do it. His sculpted his own to take her place. This piece always makes me cry.

Then off to The Forks, located at the junction of the Red and Assiniboine Rivers, which has been a meeting place for over 6,000 years. We chose the Alloway Arch, installed by The Winnipeg Foundation, to set up *Foxy David,* a sculpture of King David, who fell into a bad time when he stalked Bathsheba.

This was one of the first sculptures that Cliff had done – King David sitting on a tombstone, obviously watching someone with a spy glass. I asked him what it meant. He shrugged. "I love King David." At the preliminary hearing we had heard, for the first time, that someone had stalked our daughter.

"Do you think there is a correlation?" I asked him.

His eyes widened.

I think that was when both of us realized how instinctive his art expression was – bypassing his logic and translating, expressing his emotions into art.

We continued to the other side of the river where we could see the junction of the Red and Assiniboine Rivers – and pulled out *Jonah*, setting him up beside the river. This was the man who had a message to give but ran away, representing Cliff's running away and my struggle with words. The river flowed – symbolic of running and the force of words.

In the same location, with the Canadian Museum for Human Rights as a background, we set up an iron ball with hands popping out of it. Cliff had called it *The System* – representing the different systems that become part of every victim story. It's not only the murderer that does disabling harm, but the aftermath of murder which almost always includes loss of status, work, moving, careless living and escapism which all result in further economic losses.

Then to represent justice revictimization – we set up the *Justice Lady* on a plinth near the front doors of the Law Courts Building.

Moving to the Legislative Building, we used the imposing entrance pillars as a backdrop for the sculpture of King David with a sling in his hand but with a lamb's head. It was entitled *David and Goliath*, representing the courage needed to live after being filled with paralyzing despair.

Since we were downtown, we swung by the hotel wildly painted in black and white – by the Vineyard Church – to highlight the similarly twisted black and white DNA sculpture that represented the pursuit of truth, entitled *Nano Speck*.

Then we headed across the city and north for about eleven kilometers to Stony Mountain Institution. Knowing how closely the walls are patrolled, we went past it and found the far corner of a field where we set *Samson* on a white plinth, representing the brute strength of an offender. The symbolic fortress is in the background.

Close to the penitentiary we noticed a lovely field of sunflowers that seemed the ideal location for *Doubt* – representing the confusion of blame. It seemed the perfect place for the little man on top of the flowing blanket to ponder the question, "Who is to blame?" – amidst a field of sunflowers with their optimistic, beautiful faces.

Next to the field, a pile of rotting hay bales seemed perfect for *Fence Post* – the sculpture of a trapped man with a tortured expression, representing the cycling brain of a victim – trapped in inner pain.

Then on our way home down Kenaston Boulevard, we featured two more *King David* sculptures in Assiniboine Park. We set one in the English Gardens and the other in the Leo Mol Sculpture Garden.

One David is resting and the other is dancing – to represent the fatigue and the controversy of victimization.

The second day we drove to the Trappist Monastery Ruins in St. Norbert, very close to our own house. The ruins were the ideal place to feature the spiritual crisis inherent in any tragedy – so vividly captured in Cliff's sculpture, *The Hand of God*, which is literally a big hand with a tiny shack.

And then on the grounds of the ruins we put a few white plinths featuring the *Feathered Throne of Swords*, and the letting go of the *Feathered Hands*. We also included the feathered hands with the locket sculpture called *Friends*. Candace was all about friends. These last three sculptures, representing faith, hope and love, were spread around the lawn – as the perfect summary for the show.

At the end of day, after saying good-bye to that amazing film crew, Cliff and I paused for a glass of wine.

That's when we realized again how blessed we were.

We had just fulfilled a dream of ours.

A long time ago Cliff had proposed to me in a tiny Zephyr car with a broken heater. He had hoped to make it a special night and take me to a restaurant in Saskatoon, but it was freezing. We knew we wouldn't be able to make the hour-long drive so Cliff pulled off the road and there, on the outskirts of a little prairie town on the open prairie, beside a stubble field…with a low whisper of the wind in the background, he proposed. Shivering with the cold, together we had vowed that, since our relationship had come out of a creative project, we would continue to be creative and have fun. We had vowed that someday we would live as artist and writer.

Then, cold as we were, Cliff cemented that vow by spinning doughnuts on an icy church parking lot just to celebrate.

That dream had been overshadowed and almost lost over the years, as we raised our children, fought through our tragedy and survived our poverty.

We had just fulfilled our dream. We were surprised at the "creative high" we could still share after all these years.

It was a miracle that we were still together, that we could still partner with each other creatively and with such harmony.

As a sculptor, Cliff had fought the reptilian image with the circling tail. I had taken on my voracious, wolf-like dog by writing. Together and separately, we had dispelled that fierce, menacing, shapeshifting cloud on our bed.

Now – many, many years later – through our creativity, we could see that the word "forgiveness," our desperate social experiment, had worked.

We could raise our glasses in celebration.

Chapter 23
PECULIAR POWER

It's really all about Mount Everest – the image that came to me when having coffee with the man in the Grill 41 Restaurant and Bar.

All along, forgiveness had felt as if I was climbing a mountain. But then, after Johann Hari's visit, it felt as if I had reached a new summit.

From this vantage point, I could look back. There were no longer thunderous clouds in the sky. There were some fluffy, white clouds around but they added to – rather than took away from – the view.

It was at this new height that I reread *White Banners* – this time from a place of clarity and hindsight.

I paused when in the book, Hannah describes forgiveness. "It is the secret renunciation, the giving-up, the letting-go, the sacrifice that nobody understands…."

No wonder forgiveness is such a hard sell. At the outset it looks as if forgiveness should disempower, sideline, attract the bullies – and result in failure.

It presents itself as a less desirable door – a gray, unattractive, battered door.

Let me explain….

When we experience an injustice of a serious nature, we are given three choices: fight, flight or forgive. There are three doors – not just two!

The first two, fight and flight, come naturally to us – blind reactions, instinctive.

There is a wide path to them – and plenty of societal pressure to open them.

The third door is counter-intuitive and always demands an intentional choice to go against one's own nature and move in another direction. The path to it is full of controversy.

Opening one of the doors is only the first step.

Each door leads to a lifestyle. The first two lead to dead ends. Fight leads to a life of violence and broken relationships. It leaves a path of destruction.

Flight is another word for avoidance which usually leads to more fear – a life of timidity, anxiety and worst of all "stuckness." That dreaded word.

Both of these first two doors open to a world haunted with clouds of every kind.

However, the third door opens to a wider playing field. Forgiveness always partners with goodness and love.

Behind this third door, one is forced to overcome the trauma challenges by incorporating something positive and good – showing love instead of hate. It feels like a steep mountain climb all the way. It's hard.

Yet now when I look back the scenery from the top of the mountain, the view is breathtaking.

I read more.

Hannah continues, "...but the person who does it – that generates inside of you a peculiar power to...."

A peculiar power?

I pondered.

Had I experienced this peculiar power? Peculiar means something unusual, something distinctive – special, even odd? Unexplainable?

I had to think....

Is there a peculiar power in the desire to forgive?

Does forgiveness release miracles?

Then I see it....

Yes – there is an incidental finding to this desperate social experiment of mine. One could also call it an unintentional discovery.

It appears as if there is an invisible force behind forgiveness – a metaphysical component. There is something about the choice to forgive that draws in "the supernatural," a phenomenon that is outside everyday experience or knowledge. This peculiar power precedes the choice, accompanies the choice and then enhances the choice after.

This force draws us to the door and invites us to open the door and then awaits us behind the door.

First of all, this peculiar power becomes evident in the way it plays with time and brings about those strange coincidences that leave us in awe. Those "speak-of-the-devil" moments are a sign that the peculiar power is at play.

I'm no longer surprised when this happens.

Recently during a therapy session, as we were talking about the issues with a troublesome ex-wife, my client suddenly reached for his vibrating cellphone, and then gasped, "Speak of the devil." It's an idiom we use often when an object of distress unexpectedly becomes present during the conversation.

It often happens very dramatically when dealing with highly volatile relationships.

There are coincidences that leave one breathless.

For example, when we were organizing an encounter in Edmonton between an offender family and the victim's family at a nearby institution. We were in charge of organizing the travel for the victim family. Another organization was in charge of the offender family.

Edmonton is hardly a one-hotel kind of town, so we would never have thought that our two organizations – unbeknownst to each other – would book their clients in the same hotel. And then on top of that – the front desk booked them into two suites right across the hall from each other! Imagine that – in this huge, spacious hotel with more than a hundred rooms.

There was immediate trauma.

Offender families and victim families have the same traumatic reaction to each other as the primary victim and offender do to each other, so we had to move one of the families to another wing of the hotel.

Does this peculiar power have special interest in the reconciliation forgiveness process?

I could give you example after example, even in my own personal life.

After having a heated argument with a woman in the East, I ended it rather bitterly, never expecting to see her again. One week later, we were at a Vancouver conference together and seated at the same table – next to each other – during the opening banquet. Proximity forced us to resolve our issues.

Another example – in the case of a rape. There can't be anything more volatile. It had been a random rape outside a convenience store. The parties were unknown to one another and she would never have learned who it was until he committed another similar rape, was arrested, convicted and jailed.

She was deeply troubled and upset even with the sight of him in the media.

Then both of them experienced the death of a close family member. He obtained a special release from prison to attend the funeral. Both of these funerals were going to be held at the same funeral home at the same time.

If there hadn't been an intervention, they would most certainly have met each other in the hall at the most vulnerable moment of grief for both of them. What are the chances of that?

In this case, realizing this strange connection, both of them were motivated to settle the issues in a conversation rather than meet each other by chance. She initiated an encounter.

As I saw these stories accumulate, I asked a group of seasoned mediators if they were noticing these coincidences. Were they concerned about uncontrolled intersections between victims and offenders?

"Yes," they resounded with one voice. In fact – they had come to anticipate it – and were no longer surprised. They now assumed it could happen if they weren't careful to plan in advance to deter it. They shared the horror of exposing their clients to uncontrolled, traumatic intersections without support during or after an encounter – with the same horror that I had experienced.

Together we wondered: Why these strange coincidences? Why is there such an inexplicable power of attraction between the victim and offender? Was it linked with the peculiar power of forgiveness?

I could go on and on.

Secondly, this peculiar power is a genius match maker with a special interest in creating peace between sworn enemies. It is also interested in the magic that happens when two unlikely souls forge a connection.

Apparently, the greater the conflict, the greater the energy and opportunity if they reconcile. This force really wants us to learn to love our enemies. When we forgive and make friends of our enemies, they become our biggest teachers. Forgiveness allows us to cross borders – and create extraordinary liaisons and access unique resources.

For an example, it even allows us to work with impossible people like notorious criminals.

It allows us to have ground-breaking conversations.

Like those first breakfasts with René – we both broke through a thick, impossible barrier between us. He did as much forgiving and learning as I did. Had this peculiar power led us together to heal us?

Another example was that first inmate meeting when we were at a stalemate and the kingpin stood up and dared to say, "We aren't forgiving either." Just that simple concept with that powerful forgiveness word seemed to have a power of its own. The force of the peculiar power was evident.

There were all of those arranged Safe Justice Encounters that started with such animosity and hatred but ended with a generous effort by both parties to understand and forgive. I still marvel at the exquisite storytelling that happened during those encounters.

There was the "F-Word" Consultation of murder victims – that dissolved into a flow of healing tears at the thought of forgiving themselves.

There was the Washington taxi driver who radiated forgiveness and dispelled the darkness. A walking example of a peculiar power! It has an aura!

There were those genius proposals birthed out of two vastly different understandings of Restorative Justice.

There was the Candace House. Now I believe pixie dust is another word for peculiar power.

Thirdly, the peculiar power is one of unexpected flourishment. Yes – flourishment.

Even though forgiveness is born out of letting go and what seems like a series of sacrifices, the choice is empowering and enriching in the most mysterious ways.

Hannah in *White Banners*, who comes to the family as a domestic servant, becomes a financial advisor to her boss, an intelligent but impractical science instructor. Her forgiveness mindset helps her to see creative solutions for all of his failures. He flourishes under her influence.

I remember dismissing this part of the story as just a good plot line. What did finances have to do with forgiveness?

Then I looked at the Mennonites who have sustained a culture of forgiveness. Were they endowed with this peculiar power of flourishment?

When I took a course in Mennonite history with Dr. Harry Loewen at the University of Winnipeg, I noticed an underlying theme. It seemed that if the Mennonites escaped martyrdom, which had its own promise of reward, they would settle in a new land and flourish. Rulers of the day would take advantage and tax them heavily but they still flourished.

Then I remembered my father – making those forgiveness decisions which I thought made him a poor businessman, but later in life he came upon some quirky financial opportunities that left him very comfortable.

Then I remembered my father-in-law, a poor farmer in Borden, Saskatchewan with few opportunities except hard work, as he moved off the little farm into a janitorial position in the city. He too was an exceptionally forgiving man refusing to take offense and smiling all the time.

Throughout his life he too encountered quirky financial opportunities that left him very comfortable.

But what about us? There was no hope for us. Cliff and I are creatives, we were already destined to be starving artists. Add to that an epic tragedy, and I thought we were doomed.

Add to that the insinuation and insult that Cliff experienced when he was held a suspect in the murder of our own daughter – a suspicion so strong that he became almost unemployable.

Then out of pure desperation and ingenuity, Cliff, quite late in life, through a series of quirky opportunities developed a successful commercial cleaning business with over twenty accounts and more than fifteen staff. After a while he even broke into the world of after-construction cleaning jobs.

Together with other business ventures, we have found ourselves financially comfortable and even able to donate back to society. That in itself is a miracle.

So here I am sitting on this summit.

At this point, even though I still might not be able to define forgiveness, even though I failed the forgiveness process a million times, even though I sometimes regretted the public forgiveness stance I took, even though I might have resented the public and personal accountability that came with choosing forgiveness, I am still glad we as a couple chose the word and tried to live it out.

In some inexplicable way, it keeps the clouds at bay. It restores faith in humanity and definitely saves relationships. I believe it is essentially life giving – not life taking.

And as an eternal romantic, I would add that I am glad that I saw it all, consciously or unconsciously, as a forgiveness experiment.

Experiment implies risk. Daring – a mindset that creates excitement and amazing memories.

However, forgiveness loses its peculiar power when it is expected, manipulated or imposed. It needs to be applied creatively to each personal journey and cannot be presented as a prescribed, enforced dogma.

It serves us best when it is an adventure every step of the way.

So I do agree with Hannah now that forgiveness has a peculiar power – it attracts miracles.

In fact, I have seen more miracles in the work of restorative justice and forgiveness than I have in my work in the church.

I don't think it matters much where, who or what. It is the desire to forgive that unleashes a force of peculiar power. It is the counter-intuitive desire to take that unnatural step to make amends, to do good rather than evil, to love rather than hate – that is noticed and rewarded with extra-ordinary miracles.

There is the miracle of life in the simple gesture of forgiveness.

I guess the question now is: Would Cliff and I have been as fulfilled and creative at the end of our lives – where we find ourselves now – if we hadn't forgiven?

I don't think so. At the bedroom door, when we saw that dark, frightening presence on our bed – we chose the word forgiveness.

And I do believe it has made all the difference.

TIMELINE

1984, November 30, – at 13 years old, Candace disappears

1985, January 17, – Candace's body was found in a shed

1985, April 1, – Child Find Manitoba

1988, August 29, –Survivors support group

1992, March 12, – First Encounter – 100 inmates

1992, November, met René Durocher

1996, April 22, – René and the Lifers' Lounge

1996, November, – applied for position, Victims' Voice

1996, Stony Mountain Lifers' Group initiate the
    Candace Derksen Fund

2004, November 16, – Winnipeg Police open Project Angel
    Cold Case

2007, May 16, – Accused charged with first-degree murder of
    Candace

2009, August 24 to September 10, – Preliminary Hearing

2010, Paying Forward Project – Stony Mountain Institution

2011, January 17 to February 18, – First trial, begins 26 years later

2012, February 9, – TEDx Manitoba Presentation

2014, January 16, – Candace House Consultation

2014, November 14, – Supreme Court of Canada hearing

2017, January 16, – Second trial begins

2017, October 18, – Verdict – "Acquittal"

2018, November 26, – Candace House opens

ACKNOWLEDGEMENTS

Even though this is my story and my view of the experiences, I am fully aware that I did not live in isolation. In fact, becoming involved with the restorative justice movement in its infancy gave me the opportunity to encounter some of the best people in the world.

Without a doubt, those attracted to the philosophies of Restorative Justice are some of the least judgmental, most generous folk that I have ever met. They have the wonderful ability to cross impossible boundaries and create empathy in the most unlikely places. They are heroes – all of them. And I thank them for allowing me to enter into this amazing journey with them. I wish I could name them all, but I'm afraid to start for fear that I will leave someone out. Thank you for your understanding.

I also want to thank every program organizer that invited me to speak at their event. I was honored to be invited and learned so much from every event. I also want to thank every person attending these events, who talked to me and who asked me a question. Those questions and deep conversations pushed me to new heights of learning and expression.

I also want to thank the journalists and media hosts who interviewed me along the way and assisted me in my mandate to deepen victim awareness.

I also want to thank those who worked on our case within the justice system. It might not have ended with a conviction, but the process, the time, the care and the effort were a comfort to us. The information uncovered during the investigation and trials was extremely important to us. The consultations by the Crowns and Victim Services were an amazing support.

Putting the concept of a life experiment down on paper has been an incredible challenge I didn't expect. To this end I am indebted to my husband, Sue Simpson, Shannon Schultz, René Durocher,

Graham Reddoch, Eileen Henderson, Lois Coleman Neufeld, my children, their spouses, and many others who listened patiently as I processed this manuscript over and over and over again.

I want to thank all the fifty readers, beta readers, endorsers, and friends who provided me with valuable corrections, reflections and insights that made this manuscript so much better. I also thank them for their encouragement that gave me the courage to write my story.

But most of all I want to express my gratitude to so many fellow journeyers, my dear friends, who also experienced murder and were members of the various support groups we organized. Those times were tough, but rich with learning. I thank those who participated in all of those encounters we held. I thank all the inmates, offenders, mentors, friends and acquaintances whom I have met along the way.

I thank those who made Candace House happen.

You have, through our relationships, given me the opportunity to observe resilience at work.

With great appreciation!

Wilma

René Durocher spent 23 years of his life as an inmate in 17 different penitentiaries.

René Durocher is the recipient of the Canadian Criminal Justice Association Restoration Award, The Pierre Allard - Phoenix Award, The John Howard Society of Canada Humanitarian Service Award, The Tom French Memorial Award, and The Correctional Service of Canada Teamwork Award. He has received certificates of appreciation from the Winnipeg Police Department, the Brandon City Police Department, the United Way, the Association in Defence of the Wrongly Convicted (AIDWYC) and from the American Correction Association conference in the USA. He is an Honorary Member of the Pegasus Lifers Association.

Wilma, we share a story.
I'm glad we could be there for each other.
Sincerely,
René

Books available through:
amazon.com

INTRODUCTION BY **MALCOLM GLADWELL**
New York Times Bestselling Author

THE
WAY
OF
LETTING
GO

One Woman's Walk Toward Forgiveness

WILMA DERKSEN

Maybe it was the sting of remarks from a relative or friend. Maybe a miscarriage ended your hopes for a family. For all of your heartbreaks, maybe you wished there was someone to help you through. For Wilma Derksen, letting go of the 15 misconceptions about grief led her back to hope. In this book she tells how you can do the same.

Wilma's world collapsed when her teenage daughter, Candace, was taken hostage and murdered. Wilma now shares her choices to "let go" of heartbreak, which gave her the courage to navigate through the dark waters of sorrow. Like Wilma, maybe your heartbreak forced you to retreat from happy expectations, of believing that life is fair, of finding closure for every circumstance. She encourages patiently: let go of the happy ending, let go of perfect justice, let go of fear, and let go of closure. Wilma's wisdom will help you overcome your broken heart, and her advice will enable you to break free of pain to live a life of true joy.

Books available through:
amazon.com